WHAT DO YOU WANT MOST FROM LIFE?

You would almost certainly
say you want to be successful.
How do you attain success?
First, you need the *wisdom*
to know what to do,
the *knowledge* of how to do it,
and the *self-motivation* to do it.
Self-motivation is what this book
is all about.

The Miracle *of* Motivation

GEORGE SHINN
The action guide to happiness and success

LIVING BOOKS
Tyndale House Publishers, Inc.
Wheaton, Illinois

Living Books is a registered trademark of Tyndale House
Publishers, Inc.

Unless otherwise noted, Scripture quotations are from the
Holy Bible, King James Version.

I wish to thank my good friends Bill Eastman and Pat
Scannell for their valuable assistance in the research, writ-
ing, and rewriting of this book.

Acknowledgment is to be granted to *Success Unlimited* for
some of the true stories that appear in this book. These ac-
counts have been adapted from the following articles:

Bauman, Sam. "The Man in Black Walks the Line." *Success
Unlimited*, October 1977.

Herschensohn, Bruce. "The Marriotts: A Family's Success
Story." *Success Unlimited*, September 1977.

Olesky, Walter. "Detour for a Dead-End Kid." *Success Unlimited*, July 1977.

Stone, W. Clement. "I Read the Book . . . But Nothing Happened." *Success Unlimited*, August 1977, 6.

Williams, W. P. "Striking Gold in a Car Wash." *Success Unlimited*, November 1977.

Library of Congress Catalog Card Number 93-61222
ISBN 0-8423-3967-1

Printed in the United States of America

99 98 97 96 95
9   8   7   6

To my mother
Irene Cline Shinn

CONTENTS

AUTHOR'S NOTE

There are different kinds of motivation—internal and external motivation. Internal motivation is the same thing as self-motivation. External motivation is that which is frequently measured in experimental psychology—rats in mazes, motivation times, correlations, etc.

In *The Miracle of Motivation* we are, for the most part, dealing with internal motivation, not external motivation. For the sake of style, however, the terms *self-motivation* and *motivation* will be used throughout this book interchangeably.

We trust the reader will understand that, in any case, our subject is that "power to action" a person can draw from within himself, and that the term *motivation* should not be taken in its scientific, statistical sense.

UNIT

I

BELIEVING IN YOURSELF

ONE
What Motivation Can Do for You

What do you want most from life? You would almost certainly say you want to be successful. How do you attain success? First, you need the *wisdom* to know what to do, the *knowledge* of how to do it, and the *self-motivation* to do it. Self-motivation is what this book is all about.

What is self-motivation? I believe there are two parts to it. The first is *mental:* you conceive in your mind where you want to go. The second part is *physical:* you take action to get there. Mind and action are equally important. It's like driving a car—you have to know where you're going before you get in and start driving. Self-motivation—thought and action—is a key to success.

Observe a successful person. No sooner does he achieve his goal than he will set newer and higher goals in order to further extend his success and happiness. This does not mean that a successful person has no disappointments. But he is successful because he knows how to overcome them and get on top of them.

But the basic question is, How do you achieve the goals you have set for yourself? *How* can you be what you want to be?

That is what this book is all about: how to achieve happiness and success in life. It sets forth guidelines that have worked for others, guidelines that are simple and proven. But these guidelines work only when there is self-motivated action on the part of those who want to get ahead. They do nothing for the person who will do nothing for himself.

W. Clement Stone, founder and president of the Combined Insurance Companies of America, tells the story of an irate woman who called him to complain that she and her husband had "wasted their money" on two of Mr. Stone's books. Since Mr. Stone was out, Linda, one of his six secretaries, handled the call. The woman said, "I read those books and nothing happened. My husband is still out of work. We still have no money in the bank. I'm still standing ten hours a day—waiting tables in that crummy restaurant. Nothing happened!" The woman then quoted from one of the books, "Whatever the mind of man can conceive and believe, he can achieve."

Linda had the insight to ask, "But what action did you take as a result of reading Mr. Stone's books?" After a long pause came the woman's answer: "I waited." Linda gave the woman a bit of advice she'd often heard Mr. Stone give: "A writer of self-help action literature judges his work by what *action* the reader takes as a direct result of what he has read."

Linda then suggested that the woman read the books again, looking, not for *magic*, but for a principle or idea of particular relevance that she could follow through with action. "Maybe," Linda said, "the idea would be to further your education so that you could get a meaningful job and one that would pay better than waiting on tables in the 'crummy restaurant.'"

Several months later the woman called back. By chance she happened to reach Linda again, though the woman did not know Linda's name. The anonymous caller said, "You probably don't remember me. But a couple of months ago you suggested that I read Mr. Stone's books and do something about them—not just wait. I just had to call and tell you what happened."

As Linda had suggested, the woman had read the books again, but this time she was motivated to follow through with action. She'd gotten her husband to read the books, too, and though he was still out of work, he was diligently looking for a job. The woman herself had gone back to school, taking shorthand and typing. She'd already had three offers of jobs upon completion of her schooling—at double the income she had been earning at the restaurant.

MOTIVATIONAL MEMO

The self-motivated person pairs nouns with verbs: he determines his goals (nouns) and acts to achieve them (verbs).

The woman ended by saying, "We still have a long way to go. There are so many bills to be paid—but we're on our way. I wanted to thank you. You were right: The answers were there in Mr. Stone's books."

You too have that "bit of magic" inside you. I call it *the miracle of motivation.* But like Clement Stone's caller, you need to put the principles of this book into action.

If you want to improve your position in life, if you want to be happier and more successful, if you want to set new records, if you want to do anything at all even though it may seem utterly impossible, come with me through this book, but only if, like the woman in Mr. Stone's story, you are willing to motivate yourself and only if you are willing to move into action.

Modern life can lull a person into believing that success and happiness depend on luck.

Not so! Not so at all! You may get by on luck for a short time, but if you have not practiced the principles of motivated action, you will not know how to take advantage of whatever luck brings your way. Nor will you learn how to reach happiness and success when luck plays no part whatsoever.

The key to this book is *you!* This book will help you prepare yourself for success; it will show you what motivation can do for you. This book will convince you that health and appearance matter and will aid you in overcoming your problems. This book will direct you to develop certain skills, enable you to plan your life effectively, and instruct you in the wisest use of your time. Most of all, this book will teach you how faith—faith in yourself, faith in others, and faith in God—can help you move mountains. *But this book is worthless unless you are willing to move into action.*

Motivation is the key to successful living. This book is practical, down-to-earth. Yet it will work only for those who will motivate themselves to take positive, goal-oriented action.

Meanwhile, I'll be with you along the way to tell you true stories about how certain individuals overcame their problems and soared to new heights of success and happiness.

TWO
You Must Believe You Can

Belief is an attitude, a point of view, the way you think about something. You form attitudes through knowledge and experience. Furthermore, you can change your attitude if you motivate yourself to do so.

Perhaps you disliked a person because of a particular habit he had or because of the way he dealt with other people. Yet later your opinion became one of respect when you noticed changes in his behavior. What happened? Your attitude changed. It changed because the person changed.

So it is with your attitude toward yourself. It too can change if you change. But you have to do the changing.

Do you think of yourself as being unhappy most of the time, disorganized, unable to fulfill your dreams, always at the bottom of the ladder? It's very easy to let life get you down, to give up, for it takes more effort to be happy than to be sad. Becoming depressed and upset and giving in to feelings of despair are the easy things to do, for they require no action, no energy. But is that what you want from life? Are you happy that way? Of course not! You want opportunity!

Opportunity starts with attitude, and opportunity is everywhere if we will only create it. But your attitude must be positive if you are to create opportunity.

If you didn't have a strong desire to improve your attitude about yourself, you would not be interested in self-motivation and would not be reading this book. The fact that you see a need for self-improvement is good because
—It indicates you are honest about yourself;
—It indicates you wish to have an attitude of security and self-confidence;
—It indicates you have a desire to grow, to become a better person.

And now you can do something to bring about this new attitude. The first step is to believe in yourself.

BELIEVING IN YOURSELF

No one but you can make you believe in yourself; others can help, but you are the only one who can bring this about. Belief in one's self is the very basis of successful self-motivation. Regardless of who you are and regardless of your education or station in life, your attitude about yourself can be totally positive—if you believe in yourself. There are four things you must do that are basic to believing in yourself:

First: Make a list of the goals in your life, goals for your success and happiness—your dreams. The following are a few sample goals:
- —To get along with other people more effectively
- —To become president of the company
- —To be elected a state senator
- —To be an excellent teacher
- —To become a better parent
- —To become the best mechanic in the shop
- —To obtain a college education
- —To make a million dollars

Now arrange your goals in the order of the priority you give them; the goal you wish to reach first should be listed first. Also, put a date after each goal indicating when you desire to reach it, but be realistic about the date and the goal.

GOAL	Date	**GOAL**	Date
1.		5.	
2.		6.	
3.		7.	
4.		8.	

Second: Make a list of the steps you must take to reach your various goals. Your list might include the following: proving to your employer that you are worthy of promotion, outselling all salespeople in your company, coming up with an idea to greatly increase your company's profits, developing a way to communicate effectively with others, landing a position that will pay you more dollars per year, finishing high school with a B+ average, getting to work on time consistently, developing a habit of caring for others, eliminating a habit of peddling rumors, gaining more friends.

GOAL #1:

Step 1

Step 2

Step 3

Step 4

Step 5

Third: To reach your goals step-by-step, there are certain qualities of personal behavior that will be required of you. Again, be completely honest with yourself, and list them. You may identify ten or twenty or more, and they may include such qualities as honesty, integrity, pleasant personality, mental awareness, neatness in appearance, devotion to duty, and hard work.

Qualities I Will Need to Have
to Pursue My Goals

1.	6.
2.	7.
3.	8.
4.	9.
5.	10.

Fourth: This step requires yet another list, this one identifying those qualities you find yourself deficient in or lacking altogether, right now—today! These are qualities you must work to acquire. This is where your work starts, to conquer them and get them off this list.

Qualities in Which I Am Currently Deficient

1.	6.
2.	7.

3.	8.
4.	9.
5.	10.

Now if you have been perfectly honest with yourself while compiling these lists, you will feel better about yourself already. A good start has been made, for you now have a profile of your present self and a profile of what your goals require in relation to you.

There are many thoughts, or *mind conditioners*, to concentrate on while working to overcome the deficiencies on your fourth list. These thoughts should be repeated over and over from the moment you rise in the morning until you retire at night. Even successful people use them constantly to stay successful. People who have broken out of dire poverty to become wealthy have centered their thinking on them. Unhappy men and women whose goal was happiness have attained that goal by concentrating on them. Let's look at these mind conditioners:

1. *Think positively about all things, including yourself.* Psychologists have proven that negative thoughts destroy morale, creativity, and zest for life, and greatly

limit one's potential for development. They can even cause illness. Your degree of success will be in direct proportion to the strength of your positive thoughts.

2. *Expect the best and always do the best you can.* Constantly doing your best will make the best even better. This is positive action.

3. *Focus on your goals constantly and visualize them as being fulfilled.* Can you imagine a game of football being played without yard markers or goal lines? The team has to have an objective: to score a touchdown. The quarterback, if he is a leader, assumes he is going to score (that is, imagines his goal fulfilled). He reads the defense and executes the game plan accordingly. If he sees the opportunity for the long pass, he takes it. But if the pass defense is tight, he grinds it out, yard by yard. But his goal is the same: to score. In the same way, you should assume you will succeed and always keep your eye on the goal. And take the best route to reach that goal. Imagining that you are happy, that you are the top producer in your company (if that is your goal), will do great things to bring this about. You

will act as if you are indeed the object on which you're focusing.

MOTIVATIONAL MEMO
In order to be motivated, you must be self-confident: if *you* believe in you, others will too.

4. *Look forward.* Yesterday has gone; so have all its problems. Today is new and full of opportunities and miracles if you will but look for them.
5. *Be willing to pay the price to achieve your goals.* You can do anything you honestly aspire to and are willing to work for. But you shouldn't do foolish things, and you must not break the laws of God and man.
6. *Above all else, believe in yourself.* Believe that whatever you want, you can bring it about. With a positive attitude you open the door to opportunity. With motivation you make the most of that opportunity.

SELF-CONFIDENCE

Believing in yourself is the key to self-confidence and a calm mind. And the mind works best when calm and confident. Lack of confidence is essentially negative thinking, which produces no good.

Those of you who read my first book may remember the story of Clara, one of my students at a business school I was operating. As we did with all our graduates, we planned to assist Clara with a job interview as she was finishing up her two-year program. But Clara displayed a lack of self-confidence. The morning of her interview, she came into my office convinced she couldn't possibly do well. She was in tears and asked to call off the appointment.

Seeing how upset she was, I decided to send someone else to the interview. But before she left I told her, "I'm going to line up another interview for you tomorrow, and I want you to go to it. In the meantime, I want you to think about something: when this school sends out a student on a job interview, it's our way of saying we're proud of you and have confidence in your abilities. You don't think we'd send somebody who would make us look bad, do you? We have confidence in you, Clara. *Now all you've got to do is acquire some confidence in yourself.*"

When Clara left, I called Jim, the general manager of a company in town, who had asked me to find him a man to be trained as office manager. When he came on the line he said, "Hi, George. Have you found me a man yet?"

I said, "I'm going to send over a very capable person that I want you to interview."

Then I told him about Clara. Jim balked. He said he wanted a man he could train to be number two in the office. But I insisted: "I want you to interview this young woman as a favor to me. She's very capable, but she doesn't believe it yet. She has no confidence in herself. I think it would be good for her to have a couple of interviews just for the experience." Reluctantly, Jim agreed to a practice run.

The next morning when Clara came into my office, she wasn't nervous at all. She was smiling, confident, and overflowing with enthusiasm. As she left for the interview she declared: "I will get that job today. I have confidence, Mr. Shinn. I'm going to make you proud of me."

I didn't have the heart to tell her this was just a practice run. I said, "Better still, Clara, make *you* proud of yourself."

After she left, I was hoping Clara would gain valuable experience from the interview.

The phone rang. It was Jim. "Are you sure you sent me the right girl?" he said.

"Was her name Clara?"

"That's what she said."

"Then it was the right girl. Why?"

"Well, it didn't come out the way you described. I was expecting a timid hummingbird; the girl who showed up was full of confidence and enthusiasm. She almost broke a couple of fingers when we shook hands."

"Really?"

"I'm telling you. We talked for a few minutes. Then I asked her, 'Clara, are you a fast typist?' She said with confidence, 'Yes, sir. I can do seventy words a minute without a mistake.' So I said: 'You need good shorthand for this job.' And she said, 'I can do 120 words a minute—without a mistake.' Then I told her, 'Well, for this important position we need someone who is good in accounting.' Clara leaned up to my desk and said, 'I can open and close a complete set of books—without a mistake.'

"I couldn't believe someone with no experience could be so confident. So I asked her one more question before I hired her: 'Clara, do you lie?' She smiled, looked me right in the eye, and said, 'No sir, but I can learn!'"

Clara had done herself proud. And in the process, she'd learned something very important about self-confidence: if you look self-confident and act self-confident, you will *be* self-confident.

THREE
Discover Your Hidden Talents

You have within you an enormous number of hidden talents. Why do I say they are hidden? Because their potential is seldom used; the bulk of their power lies dormant, waiting to be used to full capacity.

There is nothing more wasteful than unfulfilled potential; it has no practical value at all until it is released from storage to become kinetic energy—energy to help you reach your goals.

Hidden talents reside in your mind—that marvelous storehouse that fills your cup to overflowing when it is tapped and exercised, the storehouse that knows no end to its bounty.

Releasing your hidden talents requires motivation on your part, motivation that will bring your talents into full use.

THE POWER OF ENTHUSIASM

Enthusiasm is one of these hidden talents. Enthusiasm is not just positive thinking, but rather the action that supports positive thinking—an inner and outer manifestation of positive thinking. Like grease on the axle of a wheel, it smooths your journey to your goals. People with whom you come in contact respond positively and enjoy your company when you are enthusiastic about yourself, your goals, about others, and about the world around you.

THE POWER OF A GOOD MEMORY

The talent of memory can also be a powerful tool if it is exercised and trained to recall names and past events with ease. Often names and past events are needed instantly. To be unable to recall them can result in losing a sale, missing an important meeting, insulting a person by calling him the wrong name, even looking stupid for failure to recall recent information you have stored in your brain. But a person who can instantly recall names, faces, and events is paces ahead of others.

How do you develop a good memory? Start with the knowledge that you will remember something *if it is really important to you.* For example, if you were to be introduced to your new boss, it is not likely you would forget his name. Why not? Because it is vitally important for you to remember it. That is the first step in memory training: you have to be *interested*.

Then, you have to *concentrate*. This means blocking out other thoughts, screening out noises, and ignoring all other outside interference. Focus only on the person or fact you wish to remember.

The next key to good memory is *repetition*—you can remember almost anything if you concentrate while repeating it over and over. If necessary, *write* it over and over. Repetition may be obvious, but it is simple and sure. It requires some effort on your part, but it does work.

Another memory aid is *association*. Association means using a prop. You try to associate or connect something with everyone you meet. With a person named Brown, you would think of the color brown. With a person named Barber, you might think of a barber pole. Some longer names may require more ingenuity in order to come up with a useful association device.

Association has its limits. Once, before an important meeting, I gave an associate of mine the names of the people who were to be there, including a Mrs. Woodhouse. After telling him how important it was that he remember her name, I gave him an association device: "Just think of the woodshed on the farm." But then, when it came time to introduce J. L. to her, I said, "Mrs. *Woodshed*, I'd like you to meet J. L. Brooks." I'd tripped over my own word association!

THE POWER OF CREATIVITY

Creativity, like memory, is a talent that can be cultivated and released to be a powerful tool in reaching your goals. To be creative does not necessarily mean to create something out of nothing or to be hit suddenly by inspiration. Creativity is often seeing the connection between two seemingly unrelated ideas or things.

For example, J. M. Haggar, founder of the Haggar Company, took Henry Ford's idea of a production line and mass-produced fine trousers at popular prices. People in the clothing industry said he'd never make it. But, using the ends of suit fabrics instead of denim, Haggar made a new kind of dress pants he called "slacks" and in the process revolutionized the clothing industry.

More recently, Leo Lauzen saw the connection between accounting services and the needs of small businesses. As a university student, he once asked a professor why he always used illustrations that dealt with large companies worth millions of dollars. Lauzen wanted to know who did the accounting for small business firms.

Lauzen found a way to take care of the accounting needs of small businesses, founding Comprehensive Accounting Corporation. Later, Lauzen saw the connection between two more ideas: his accounting service for small businesses and the franchising concept.

If you wait until the creative urge hits you, or until inspiration hits, you will probably wait a very long time. Whatever the problem is, try to solve it with your conscious mind before asking for help. The more you use creativity, the more it delivers for you, and the more its use becomes automatic. And sometimes your most creative thoughts come to you while working, a spin-off of the very work you are doing.

Constantly releasing your mental powers through creativity can become a habit—so much so that answers and solutions will come to you constantly, speeding you toward your own personal goals.

Creativity can have a very wonderful by-product called *serendipity*. Serendipity is discovering something totally unrelated to the problem you are trying to solve. For example, Columbus discovered America while searching for a route to India. It is said that the American Indians, finding no water for cooking, tapped a maple tree and made the first maple syrup as the sap boiled down. Pioneers, traveling westward, stopped for water and found gold nuggets in the stream. These are all examples of serendipity.

So be on the lookout for serendipity in your life; it can be a miracle by-product of your own creative processes, and like miracles, it pops up everywhere.

THE POWER OF THE SUBCONSCIOUS

One of the most amazing and helpful aspects of the human brain is the subconscious mind. The conscious is the mind we all know; it does our thinking, it registers what we see; it helps us reason, form opinions, and make decisions. The subconscious mind is a veritable computer—a storehouse of all the information taken in by our conscious mind. All our past experience is stored there. So is what we have learned.

And it is the world's best problem solver, providing it is used properly. The more it is used, the more efficient it becomes, and the more efficient you will become using it.

MOTIVATIONAL MEMO
You can think positive thoughts all your life; you can read books on positive thinking all your life; you can go to school and get your B.A., M.A., and Ph.D.; you can have great

ability, many contacts, and abundant knowledge—but you will never become what God expects of you until you act. *And that is motivation!*

For the subconscious mind to produce the solution to a problem, it must first be triggered by the conscious mind. In other words, the conscious mind must focus on the problem so the subconscious mind will have a clear picture of what the problem is. Next, the conscious mind must have a strong desire for a solution to this problem. The stronger the desire, the greater the signal to the subconscious to act. And the conscious mind should desire in positive terms, since negative thoughts create nothing but more negative thoughts.

After the conscious mind has tried to solve the problem and has failed, and when it has defined the problem in positive terms and has also established a strong desire for a solution, it should then forget the matter entirely. Let the subconscious take it over. With its limitless ability to create and in its own time, it will analyze the problem and, sometime when you are relaxed and least expecting it, will flash a solution to the conscious mind.

Unlike the conscious mind, the subconscious is always working—during your waking hours and while you are asleep. Many a person has had a solution come to him while being totally relaxed or during sleep. Sometimes answers come swiftly; at other times it takes longer.

But there must always be a well-defined problem you wish to plant in the subconscious mind and a strong desire for a solution after you have first used all your creative and conscious efforts to solve the problem.

John K. Williams, in his book *The Knack of Using Your Subconscious Mind*, lists many discoveries that have been the result of subconscious activity. The following excerpt mentions people who were occupied with their hobbies and totally relaxed from the thoughts of their problems when their subconscious flashed an answer. Note, too, that these people are from all walks and levels of life.

> The father of photography was an army officer; and of the electric motor, a bookbinder's clerk. The inventor of the telegraph was a portrait painter; and of the jacquard loom, a dressmaker. A farmer invented the typewriter; a poet, the sewing machine; a cabinetmaker, the cotton gin; and a coal miner, the locomotive. The telephone was the after-school work of a teacher of the deaf; the disc talking machine, the night work of a clothing salesman; the wax cylinder phonograph, a

lawyer's clerk; the typesetting machine, a grocery man. A physician made the first pneumatic tire because his little son was an invalid.

RELEASING REQUIRES ACTION

Your mind has powers ready to release for your constructive use through enthusiasm, memory, creativity, and the subconscious. But in reality you are the one who has to release these powers—you, through motivation. The mind won't do it for you. You must set goals and mentally focus on them and see them being actualized. (How similar to your need for having goals to focus on is the need of the subconscious to have goals before it can act.) And through positive thinking you can create enthusiasm, develop memory, solve problems through creativity, and with your subconscious, move mountains. The results you obtain will be in direct proportion to the efforts you are willing to expend to reach your goals. If you so desire and act accordingly, nothing is impossible.

FOUR
Get Excited about Life

To get what you want from life—success, happiness, achieving your personal goals—you and you alone are responsible. Friends and loved ones may be helpful, but the responsibility is yours.

Earlier, I said a basic requirement to achieving your goals is positive thinking, but that positive thinking must be fired up for action. The spark is enthusiasm. The degree of your motivation is in direct proportion to the amount of enthusiasm you possess.

WHAT IS ENTHUSIASM?
When we think of enthusiasm, we often think of the rah-rah spirit of a football game where the spectator is a "fan"—a short form of "fanatic." The trick is to develop that same enthusiasm about reaching our goals—to become "fanatics" about life. That spirit,

properly nurtured, directed, and sustained, can help us achieve our goals. Think of enthusiasm as an attitude, a mental point of view, that excites and exhilarates with intense fervor; with it, you become truly alive, involved, and turned on. *Enthusiasm* means "full of God" or "God in you."

There is nothing more boring than a dull TV show or a game played with no intensity. They remind us of a soft drink without bubbles. But add zest and excitement to these, and what happens? The TV commands our complete attention, and the game brings us to our feet.

Life, like a soft drink, must have zest to be enjoyed. People, to be successful, must be excited about life.

Look at the enthusiasm with which a healthy, happy child approaches life. It's a sad fact that too many of us lose that zest along the way, for whatever reason. We can sometimes recapture it for a few minutes, as at a ball game. But the world belongs to the person who can keep that fire burning all the time.

Enthusiasm is an attitude of curiosity, confidence, and expectation, along with a bit of risk and daring.

WHAT YOU CAN DO WITH ENTHUSIASM
The list of what you can do with enthusiasm is endless, but let's look at a few items from such a list.

Enthusiasm changes problems to challenges. Richard Prentice Ettinger, founder of one of the world's largest and most successful publishing houses, always believed that "everything happens for the best." Whenever crises arose, they did not become problems, they became challenges—challenges that solved the crises and elevated his employees and his company to greater efficiency and productivity. Even when this great man developed cancer, he still believed that "everything happens for the best." From that point on, he took better care of his health and extended his life span beyond what it would normally have been.

Enthusiasm creates enthusiasm in others. Enthusiasm is contagious. It motivates and inspires others to the same degree that you have it. When you work with another person, you both respond to the effects of enthusiasm.

Enthusiasm ventilates the mind. Enthusiasm rids the mind of worries, tension, and fretting. The mind that is not ventilated can destroy its own ability to think straight and be creative.

Enthusiasm improves self-knowledge. Since enthusiasm and positive thinking work together, they can help you analyze your own self by identifying your strengths and weaknesses. They then help you to exercise your strengths and overcome your weaknesses.

Enthusiasm brings realization to your goals.

Enthusiasm recognizes that all things are possible and that you can bring your dreams to pass. It is fuel for self-motivation.

ORGANIZING FOR MAXIMUM RESULTS

To get maximum results from enthusiasm, you must organize for it. Organizing will help enthusiasm become automatic—a habit. Here are ways to go about it:

—Forget yesterday's failures and mistakes. Be enthusiastic about today.

—Make a list of things you wish to accomplish today and go at them with enthusiasm.

—Focus! Envision yourself achieving your goals. Believe that they are going to be realized and you have taken the most important step.

—Remember, the tougher the problem, the more enthusiasm is needed.

—Stop occasionally and take stock of yourself. Review the steps you must take to achieve your goals and the time limits set for climbing those steps. How well are you doing? Are you trying hard enough? How can you improve?

—Reward yourself. As you reach certain steps toward your goals, find some way to reward yourself. Go out for dinner or buy yourself a new tennis racquet or something else you've been wanting.

—Keep believing you can do anything you set your mind on. Think enthusiastically!

MOTIVATIONAL MEMO

An enthusiast is a fanatic about life. And because the enthusiast has the attitude that good things will happen, good things *do* happen.

Think of action as the motor of self-motivation. Enthusiasm is the oil for that motor. When there is no enthusiasm, rust sets in together with all the other problems of nonuse. But, with enthusiasm, positive thinking is actualized, goals are reached and exceeded, and life is fulfilled. Self-confidence is strengthened, and you are ready to take on the world.

Tonight, thank the Almighty for life and all its blessings. Then put all of your problems out of your mind. Relax and go to bed. In the morning, get up with the attitude that it will be a great day and that no matter what problems come your way, you have the confidence, ability, and *enthusiasm* to deal with them.

FIVE
Keep Growing

The one constant thing in life is change. Change is everywhere: in our environment, in the natural world, in the way we do things, in the way we act and react, in our thinking, in our beliefs, and in our codes of conduct. How we generate change, what we do with change, and how we react to it, determine whether we grow or fail.

GROWTH AND CHANGE
In spite of the fact that change is constant, there is nevertheless a strong tendency to resist it. Change presents an unknown factor in our lives and activities. Even though we may have problems, we are often tempted to maintain the status quo rather than venture into the unknown; that way we feel more secure and things of the past seem more predictable, more

manageable. What happens then? We isolate ourselves as much as possible from the impact of change, trying to live with the problems that we feel "safer" with even though they may make us unhappy. In other words, we become specialists in negative thinking, living selfishly to minimize the possible impacts that could bring on imagined new problems with which we are not sure we could cope.

Where does this kind of thinking get us? Nowhere! Nowhere at all!

To participate in change is to grow. Nothing grows that does not change. We watch the tiny blade become a tall grass, the bud become a flower, the egg hatch into a bird, and the child become an adult. The very act of living is change and growth.

And those who accept and adjust to change and keep growing are the winners, the successful—the fittest. Those who cannot accommodate change do not grow; they die by the wayside a mental, physical, or spiritual death.

Even nature proves that accommodating growth can be difficult. We watch the plant breaking through the earth's hard crust and pushing away a stone to make way for its leaves and flowers. The very nature of meeting these difficulties strengthens the plant and encourages it to survive. Without its ability to overcome difficulties it would die by the wayside.

Nature has a goal for the plant—to grow and bring forth blossoms that will bear seeds to produce descendants for generations to come. We have to imagine that it longs for problems to challenge it in order that its strength will increase and its offspring will survive for many generations. It becomes one of the "fittest."

The plant is not much different from you and me. We have to have goals, and we have to accommodate ourselves to change even though this means meeting problems head on, for this is growth, growth that strengthens us to become the "fittest."

The desire to grow must come from within. The plant has no cheering section urging it to push up the stone in its way, but it is compelled to do so alone if it is to grow and survive. Similarly, we must grow to survive despite obstacles, and, like the plant, we must do it ourselves. Urgings from our friends encourage us, but the task of growing is ours, and we cannot avoid it.

Genuine growth means having the courage and confidence to try new things, and in the process, to let go of worn and outdated ones, the way a tree sheds its leaves to make way for new growth. Certainly, growth involves risks, and sometimes the prospects appear frightening, so uncertain are we of what lies ahead. I am not suggesting you take foolish risks. But use the past to build on what you know is secure. Go from the known to the unknown; yet, at the same time tune yourself in on the interesting things in life and the excitement that lies ahead. No, growth is not always easy; at times it can be quite painful. Is it worth it? Well, you can choose to merely exist, leaning on others for survival. Or you can struggle and grow; you can live, *really live*, all your life.

GROWTH AND SUCCESS

Success is commonly thought of as the culmination of an activity with a "happy ending." For some reason, success and "happy endings" always seem to go together, when in reality success is but a milestone on a journey that should never end.

A "has been" is someone who was once successful but who no longer has any credentials for the present day. He has nothing to offer; he has given up. Nobody's success lasts forever. Who, except sportsmen, are interested in crossing the Atlantic Ocean in a boat as small as the one Columbus used? Or in a replica of the Mayflower? We want to cross it quickly— probably in about seven hours or less—and then get on with something else. Wilbur and Orville Wright would hardly remember their first successful flight if they were alive today to watch the satellite leaving its pad on its way to

Mars or Jupiter or even beyond. As important as Columbus, the Pilgrims, and the Wright brothers were to our history, time and change have passed by their successes. They would be the first to admit it.

Any success we achieve can be superseded, and will be, more quickly than we like to admit. We, therefore, can become "has beens" almost as soon as we have succeeded at something unless we constantly have new goals and dreams. Far too many people retire mentally after achieving a degree of success, and their claim to fame is forgotten because they have nothing else to offer. Compare them to someone like Indiana University swimming coach Doc Counsilman, who, at the age of fifty-eight, became the oldest person ever to swim the English Channel. Or to Gordie Howe, who in his early fifties was still playing in the National Hockey League, competing against men half his age who couldn't beat him out of a job. Or to S. I. Hayakawa, who, after a successful tenure as president of San Francisco State University, facing compulsory retirement, "retired" to get elected to the United States Senate at the age of seventy. Senator Hayakawa's philosophy of growth: "It seems to me that when you cease to be able to face change, that is when you really become old. I guess what I like about compulsory retirement is that it almost forces you, if you are a man or woman of spirit, to do the things you never had the time to do. At sixty-five you should be able to give up your security blanket." One man of spirit who exemplifies Senator Hayakawa's philosophy is businessman Roy Smith of Costa Mesa, California, who at age eighty-six started an insurance agency and in the second year of operation wrote over a million dollars worth of insurance. All of these men and others like them took risks, encountered resistance, and succeeded. And Senator Hayakawa is right in another regard: most successful people live long, productive lives; Grandma Moses, John D. Rockefeller, Thomas Edison, and J. C. Penney are but a few examples.

TAKING TIME TO GROW

We have said much about action in previous chapters of this book. But by contrast, there is another type of action that is needed—being alone to take stock of yourself. This, too, is part of growing up.

Periodically, businesses take a management audit to determine which of their products are selling. Are they making a profit? Are they moving ahead? Or are they falling behind in their forecasts and expectations? Accountants are called in to examine the records of the businesses to determine if their financial conditions are healthy or if the companies are losing their standing within the industry. Will they face bankruptcy if immediate changes are not made? The current status of the companies is measured against their goals and forecasts. This is self-examination.

MOTIVATIONAL MEMO
The self-motivator has a thirst for growth. He or she realizes that growth means change and change involves risks, stepping from the known to the unknown.

So it should be with people. There must be self-examination if you are serious about setting and meeting goals. There must be a time to get to know yourself and to evaluate how you are doing.

Honest reflection is a useful activity, but there is no point in such reflection if you are not interested in being absolutely realistic. This is an occasion to reappraise your progress, to review what you have learned, to decide if goals should be changed, and to reorder your priorities. It is an occasion to audit your total self and to take pride in the fact that you may have done things you never before thought possible.

What, if anything, is holding you back, and what will you do about it? Are you having trouble shedding old habits, are you "bugged" by past mistakes? This is a time to apply positive thinking and convince yourself that the past is water under the bridge, yesterday is gone forever, and it is what you do today and tomorrow that matters.

People often have a need in the quiet of their own thoughts to see themselves as worn out, as having exhausted their resources, as having used up everything they have, and then by contrast, to look at the possibilities that are untapped. It is like drilling a well to an overflowing energy reserve, like finding a bank account that has never been drawn from.

Accountants use an interesting device known as the T-account. On the left side of the T are listed assets—things you own, such as your car, house, and so forth. On the right side, liabilities or debts—what you owe—are listed. Then each column is totaled. If the liabilities exceed the assets, there could be trouble, but if the assets are more than the liabilities, then the account is safe. The more assets the better.

We should do a periodic T-account of ourselves, listing our liabilities (such as fears, doubts, handicaps, negative feelings about ourselves) and then listing our assets (abilities, valuable experiences, talents, friends, knowledge). How do we balance out? So often the personal T-account is all you need to lift you out of the doldrums. And even when the liabilities outweigh the assets, you will have an honest account of your needs and a place to start improving.

The end-products of self-reflection are fourfold:

—It reassures us of the direction we are going, which is more important than where we are today.
—It helps us shed yesterday's problems and other useless baggage that may be weighing us down.
—It reestablishes our priorities, for nothing is done until it becomes priority number one.
—It reactivates us into giving life all we have got.

THE LEARNING PROCESS

It is interesting to watch a baby grow from infancy to childhood. He is constantly reaching for things outside his immediate grasp: his food, a toy, an animal to play with. And all the time there are obstacles in his way: a table that is too high, a ball that rolls away when he touches it, a puppy that runs into another room. But still the infant continues to try, even while he is frustrated to tears. Children never give up when they are not able to do something; they believe in themselves, they know they can, they have no doubts. And they usually do what they set out to do. This is a simple learning process at work.

The learning process of an adult is somewhat more complicated. He recalls events and experiences that raise doubts. He allows himself to become affected by ridicule. He remembers the sad experience of his friends. He is tempted to give up.

Only when he stops to reevaluate his wants does he regain the simple learning process of the small child, for even as his reasons for stopping become more numerous and complicated, so do his reasons for going ahead.

We can learn a good lesson by watching the jogger. Jogging is much different from walking. When a person walks, he usually takes his time, he stops to look at views, to chat with passing friends, to wipe away perspiration if the day is hot. But not the jogger. He moves right along with a rhythm, stopping for nothing—not for the view, for friends, or to wipe away perspiration. In fact, he wants to perspire, for he is exercising. Without undergoing some strain, he would not be exercising. He is building up his body. He seeks constantly to improve himself, which takes more work and even more pain.

Now, the jogger doing his workout is similar to you and me trying to reach our goals. We've got to expect to strain a little. Maybe we're not out of breath, and we don't have tired muscles and rain in our faces, but we have other problems to overcome; these are part of our exercise.

And the more often we strain, the more often we become capable of reaching whatever we have set before us. Doing only what comes naturally gets us nowhere. This is not growth. Growing is reaching, reaching with all the stretch you've got.

PREPARE YOURSELF

Every job or profession has a set of tools that are peculiar to its special kind of work. They were invented because they make tasks easier and because they make the user more confident. And for many of these activities, the tools lighten the work until it becomes almost fun. The mason has his level and trowel, the baker his cooking utensils and his oven, the doctor has a stethoscope and various other instruments, and the salesperson has record books and a catalog of the products he sells.

As a self-motivator you need certain tools as well: positive thinking, self-confidence, common sense and intuition, specific goals, the use of your hidden talents, and a desire to grow with change. These are also our tools of growth, all of which are kept sharp through use.

II

LOOKING, FEELING, AND ACTING YOUR BEST

SIX

Cultivate Good Health Habits and Increase Your Energy

You need energy for successful motivation. Energy is like the propellant that goes into a satellite to provide thrust (action), like the gasoline that powers our cars. But the amount of energy an individual has to expend is not measured in gallons; it is measured by the condition of the human body and mind.

The first person to break the four-minute mile was Dr. Roger Bannister, a physician. He described fitness as "a state of mental and physical harmony which enables someone to carry on his occupation to the best of his ability and great happiness."

WHAT IS HEALTH?
WHO IS RESPONSIBLE FOR IT?

Health is a person's physical and mental state. When we speak of "good health," we mean that one's condition is in a satisfactory state. Conversely, "poor health" means that a temporary or permanent form of illness has lowered one's energy and prevented one from doing all he could do in "good health."

To act right, you must feel right. Healthy thought is produced in a healthy body, and a sound body will reward you with energy, optimism, harmony, and happiness.

I have noticed that successful people have one thing in common—energy. Their age makes no difference. They got that energy because they *themselves* took care of their minds and bodies. And, sadly, I have seen many people at the very point of reaching their goals fail to do so because they became victims of ill health.

I do not mean to imply that a person who has a physical handicap cannot be successful. History has too many examples to the contrary (Steinmetz, Beethoven, and Helen Keller, for example). Such people were so successful in rising above their handicaps that they completely overcame their afflictions.

For many years a common belief has been that a doctor should be in charge of a person's health. This idea is changing. A doctor can do just so much. He can advise you what to do, and he can prescribe what you need when illness strikes. But it is unrealistic to believe he can watch over you day-by-day, seeing to it that you get the proper amount of exercise or checking on your food intake to be sure that you have a well-balanced diet. That is your responsibility. And you have to be *motivated* to want good health and energy. It's easy to make excuses for overeating, drinking too much, lack of exercise, or smoking. It takes self-discipline to avoid such habits that contribute to poor health.

The idea behind the holistic health movement is that you are responsible for your own well-being, and that total health involves not only the body but the mind and spirit. The holistic approach to health recognizes that each person is different, and that it behooves each of us to discover the best way to achieve peak condition in body, mind, and spirit.

THE MEDICAL CHECKUP

If the body is intended to provide maximum vigor, good muscle tone, strength, resistance to disease, and top performance at all times, the place to start is with a medical checkup (preventive care). An annual physical examination is well worth its small investment. This is the opportunity to prevent problems and to catch would-be problems before they become major, to obtain advice about diet and weight, to obtain assurances that the heart and other organs are functioning properly, and, if not, to find out what corrective steps are needed.

Choose a doctor in whom you have complete faith, one who is current on medical research and technology. Then stick with this doctor and follow his advice. Don't be like some people who make a fetish out of going from one doctor to another if they don't like what the first one advises. Find a doctor whom you trust and stay with him. And anytime you have sudden health changes, check with him; he will have your records and be in a position to help you.

Each year in the United States total employee absences from work approximate billions of hours due to illness. Imagine the amount of productivity lost, the number of ideas that are never generated, and the dislocation of other employees that result from such absences. Because of this, our company, like many others, encourages our key people to have regular physical examinations to reduce the risk of absence because of illness.

Dental examinations should also be undertaken at least annually with a dentist whom you trust.

NUTRITION AND DIET

What our bodies take in for nourishment and for replacing worn-out tissues should be a matter of concern to everyone. While there are areas where agreement is lacking, researchers in nutrition concur on many things. For instance, there is irrefutable evidence that smoking is bad for the body, not to mention the fact that it offends many people. (Personally speaking, I feel so strongly that I consider a smoker a poor health risk and, therefore, a bad investment.) Drug and alcohol abuse are also undeniably harmful. Research seems to indicate that sugar and salt can be very harmful if they are used more than sparingly. Kinesiologists (those who specialize in the study of human muscular movements) can demonstrate immediate loss of strength in the muscles of those who take in even a small amount of sugar. There is strong evidence that bodies need certain vitamins, proteins, amino acids, grains, and bulk fibers to stay in good condition. There is general agreement that overweight can be very bad, especially for the heart, and that certain foods, such as fatty meats, can contribute to clogging the arteries.

It is a foolish person who will reject these findings that doctors and researchers agree on. But whether oatmeal is good for you and whether you feel vitamin C prevents colds are some of the subjects on which experts disagree, and you will have to experiment and find out for yourself how your body responds.

Overweight is generally the result of overeating, or just consuming too many calories. Overweight is a major contributor to heart and vascular diseases. Losing weight is extremely difficult for most people to do. And later, keeping the weight off is even more difficult. But there are thousands of people who have been successful at both—losing weight and then keeping it off. So it can be done.

Austin Harris, executive vice president of Miami Jacobs Junior College, lost over one hundred pounds. He motivated himself by keeping pictures of himself everywhere, including on the refrigerator door. To help keep the weight off, Austin still carries that picture of his formerly fat self. Fewer calories—simply eating less—was the key for Austin. Unless you have an unusual medical problem, you can lose weight by eating less, too. But do not go on a diet without seeing your doctor first. Exercise can help speed weight loss, but exercise alone probably won't do it. (I once lost about thirty-eight pounds, most of it fairly quickly. Regular exercise certainly helped, but I couldn't have done it without dieting, too.) Thinking positively about losing weight can help lighten the burden of doing so and speed you to your goal.

EXERCISE AND RECREATION
The purpose of a race horse is to win races. But would you bet on a horse that was never

exercised? Of course, you wouldn't. You recognize that exercise is necessary for the well-being of the animal to keep it in top-notch physical condition. Yet many of us take better care of our animals than we do of ourselves.

Exercise is even more important for humans than it is for animals, for a human's normal activity is mental, not physical like an animal's. And exercise not only tones up the body; it also tones up the mind.

The annual vacation is not the only time when one should exercise. Exercising should be planned for several times a week, or better still, daily. Whether you decide to swim, bicycle, play tennis, racquetball, or jog, work out a plan that puts all else aside so you can exercise several times a week at specific hours. Be faithful to those times you set aside for exercise, let nothing interfere with them; exercise is too important to become hit or miss.

There are many books on the subject of exercising. The ones that make the most sense and have done the most for me are Kenneth Cooper's books on aerobics. If you are thinking of starting an exercise program, Cooper's books can show you how to measure your fitness, how to set up a program, and how to measure your progress. And you can choose from a variety of activities, from jump rope to swimming to running to rowing.

Exercise should stretch your muscles, involve a little strain, develop deep breathing, clear the mind, cause some sweat, and make you feel good all over when it is finished. There are even exercises you can do if you are unable to go outside (calisthenics, isometrics). And don't confuse exercise with a game such as golf, which rates close to the bottom insofar as valuable exercise is concerned, although it may be enjoyable recreation. The payoff is cardiovascular fitness, which can reduce the risk of heart attack. There is also a tremendous psychological boost in exercise: worries and problems seem to evaporate during a good workout.

Good diet and exercise are without doubt the two most important factors that contribute to well-being, youthfulness, and long life. And one is never too old to begin an exercise program. C. L. Jenkins, president of our foundation, has had two heart attacks and other ailments, but Jenk, who is seventy-three, gets up and walks a brisk two miles every morning—perfect aerobic exercise for him.

At your annual physical, be sure to discuss exercise with the doctor. Ask him what he recommends for you. Whatever exercise program you choose, it's best to check with your doctor first.

While recreation is not necessarily exercise, it should be a part of your daily routine.

Take time away from the serious and strenuous duties of the day and relax. Develop interests that add more to you and your life, whether they be music, golf, gardening, camping, fishing, or painting. Free yourself completely from the serious work of earning a living with short "vacations" that "charge the batteries" and broaden the dimensions of your life. The best definition of recreation is an analysis of the word itself: "re-creation" through recreation.

MENTAL HEALTH

I have no doubt the old adage "Worry kills more people than disease" is absolutely true. Worry is a real killer; worry saps strength, causes people to be random in their work and thinking, breeds anger and confusion, and breaks up many friendships because of irritation and frustrations.

In substance, worry is caused by one's inability to see a successful solution to a problem.

What to do about worry and anxiety? There are two basic things: make a list of your worries, then analyze them. Once they are written down, many will seem small if you list them in order of their size. And still others will disappear completely when you realize that there are people who have far greater problems to worry about than you have. Worries that remain need a good dose of positive thinking to clear them from your mind.

MOTIVATIONAL MEMO
Self-motivated action occurs only when you have a pool of energy to draw from. Therefore, your success will depend on your health, your fitness, your mental well-being, and the amount of rest you get.

Who has the right to have more worries than the president of the United States? He is beset with really major problems each day, many of which have no immediate solution at all. And his problems are far more complicated than those most of us have. Yet, President Truman said he was always able to shed his problems when he retired and go directly to sleep. How could he do that? Because he had *confidence* in himself. He knew if he was doing each day the very best he could, that was all he could do. And there was nothing to worry about. What more could he ask than for God's help, which he did. Self-confidence, knowing that you have done your very best and having faith that things will work out can destroy any worry no matter how great the problem.

But, admittedly, there are times when even that is hard to do. And sometimes you need to condition yourself to have confidence and faith. There are things you can do that will help. One is to look at the problems of others; then compare those to yours. How lucky you may be to have such few and small ones! Involve yourself in doing things for others; this also destroys worry. Visit some lonely or ill person, help a handicapped person to do errands, or visit someone who is bereaved. Spend some time with nature looking at the buds as they burst into full bloom, admiring the changing color of a sunrise or sunset, or listening to the splashing of water over the rocks. Spend time with hobbies and other forms of recreation that soothe the mind. Listening to music has been so successful that an entirely new field of music therapy has achieved professional status. And meditation has successfully relaxed minds for centuries.

SPIRITUAL HEALTH

Today, more than at any other time, people are realizing that spiritual health has a direct impact on both physical and mental health. Faith in God who works for good, who has love and compassion for individuals, and who has given order to the universe, contributes to a well-ordered person. Faith is the basis of self-confidence; faith cancels out fretting and anxiety. Those with little faith in God have little chance of tapping God's healing powers for their minds and bodies.

PROFESSIONAL HELP

If one cannot overcome severe mental stress through one's own efforts, a doctor should be consulted, for if anxiety is not conquered, it will sooner or later destroy one's personality and physical health. And if your doctor advises seeing a psychiatrist for specialized help, that, of course, is the thing to do. Seeing a psychiatrist should bear no stigma whatsoever. This is a professional branch of healing, as important as medicine and surgery, and if the mind is in need of help or preventive attention, one should cooperate and use a psychiatrist as a source of healing. Just as cancer can be stopped through prompt medical treatment, so can mental problems.

REST

When you look about you, you will observe that there are few things in nature that do not require rest. What is true for nature is also true for our body. To keep from being burned out, the body must have time to rest. And while it is resting, it is also working, recharging, and healing itself to be ready to release more energy when awakened.

We sometimes try to ignore the needs of our

body and eliminate or reduce the periods of rest it requires. Eventually, however, the body will signal trouble unless it has the rest it needs.

Some people need more rest than others do. This is something each person must figure out for himself. But to cheat the body of its requirements can only bring harm.

Regular sleeping hours should be adhered to as closely as possible, and when a significant amount of sleep has been lost, it should be made up as soon as possible.

THINK HEALTHY THOUGHTS

Nothing will guarantee that you will be without sickness. But if you think healthy thoughts, pray for a healthy body and mind, and start acting healthy, your situation will most definitely improve.

Think healthy thoughts. Healthy thinking is an energy-building process. Healthy, positive thoughts will help to keep your body in balance and operating at top performance. Do not let personal or business problems make your body ill. Think defeat, and you will tend to create the circumstances that lead to defeat. But if you think success, you will create circumstances that lead to success. Focus on your mind and body as being strong and vital, and they will react to that image.

Pray for a healthy mind and body. When you

pray, put all thoughts of self out of your mind; put yourself completely under the will of God. Prayer is your way of offering yourself to God. Praying will help any sufferer to find new strength and healing.

Act healthy. You can think healthy and pray healthy, but you must do your part, too. You must act healthy. This means taking charge of your own well-being.

SEVEN
Make Appearance an Asset

When you go into a store to buy some fresh fruit or vegetables, which ones do you select? Why the best-looking ones, of course. And haven't you seen people reject a copy of the Sunday paper because there was a rip in the front page?

People want the best, whether it be fresh fruit, a bouquet of roses, or a new employee for the company. Appearance is all-important because it communicates something. Later you may discover than an apple is sour, the roses didn't last long, and the prospective employee was not really qualified for the job. But the first impression got your attention.

Since you only have one chance to make a good first impression, you must motivate a good first impression. It is to your advantage to pay careful attention to your appearance.

The first impression a person must make is to look successful. How proud I am of my associates! Our people are aware of the importance of a good personal appearance, and many times I have been complimented on how professional my people look, and how confident they act. They look and act professional because they dress and feel professional. The well-dressed person will add to his or her self-confidence and courage, and the careless and poorly dressed person will seldom make any great progress on the road to success.

FEELING RIGHT

As I have said before, to act right, you have to look right and feel right—you must have confidence that you are "in tune" with those around you. After all, you depend on others for your success socially and professionally, and your job, if you are going to be successful at anything, is to influence other people. So it is to your advantage to be dead certain that others respond to you positively, and you won't be treated as a professional unless you look and act like a professional.

But back to the fresh fruit! If you should be allowed only one of two different apples, which one would you select? Of course, you would select the better looking one. So will everybody else if they have to select between you and your competition; they will select the one who makes a better appearance.

Looking right and feeling right are dependent on outward appearance and on inward appearance or, in other words, your grooming and your personality. This chapter will concern grooming, and we'll discuss personality in the following chapter.

THE BASICS OF A GOOD WARDROBE

When it comes to good grooming, what is correct? Who sets the standards? If you meet ten people in one day, you can see up to ten different outfits that they are wearing. Some may be very casual, others quite formal. Perhaps some will even appear to you to be a bit strange. How, then, do you know what to wear?

The key is appropriateness. How you dress depends on the occasion, whether it's a football game, a family picnic, or a business meeting. Clothing runs the gamut of styles. Some styles give the impression of being underdone, others of being overdone, but in between there is always a happy medium that is neither too extreme nor too conservative.

MOTIVATIONAL MEMO
To act right, you have to look right and feel right.

Do not be concerned if you are limited in the

amount you are able to spend for clothes, but buy the best quality you can afford. No one is going to feel your garments to see if they are of the best quality. People can look good in garments that cost much less if they fit well and are neatly pressed. The important thing is to look neat, no matter what you pay for your clothes. You determine what is best for you. Shop around, if necessary. And if you are not sure of what's best for you, find a book on proper dress.

SPECIFICS ON GOOD GROOMING

Clothes should be comfortable and fit properly. Seek advice on this if you are unsure of yourself. Suits and dresses should be tasteful, pressed, and clean. For men's dress shirts, my personal preference is white—white is always right, as the saying goes. A white shirt looks good with any suit, and it looks professional. But again, *how you dress should be appropriate for the occasion and the job.*

Shoes should be kept shined and in good repair. Keep your nails clean and neatly trimmed. If you have a problem with skin irritations, get medical help if necessary. If you wear glasses, make sure the frames suit your face, and keep your glasses clean. And don't forget to take off sunglasses when you are inside. Most people prefer to look you squarely in the eye when talking to you, and colored lenses prevent this. I have a tendency to discredit what a person tells me when he or she is wearing dark glasses.

How about hairstyle? True, it's a free country and you can wear your hair the way you want. But if you want to get ahead, you will want to avoid extremes in hairstyles. As with other matters of appearance, a bizarre or extreme hairstyle focuses attention on itself rather than on *you*. (A tip for men: Many companies favor a clean-shaven, short-haired look for their male employees. If so, this is a small price to pay for a position you really want. Again, the key is appropriateness.) Hair, regardless of style, should always be clean and combed. If you have dandruff, control it with medicated shampoo and brushing.

THE "UNTOUCHABLES"

Avoid nervous habits or mannerisms, such as chewing gum, smoking, rubbing your face, talking too loudly.

Avoid careless diction or grammar. The kind of language we use in a football game may not be appropriate for the boardroom or dinner table. We are often judged, fairly or not, on how we use the English language. It takes a great deal of effort to learn standard English usage, but the effort is worth it because it enables us to use the language with precision and to communicate our ideas clearly and concisely.

One of the problems with avoiding some of these bad habits or "untouchables" is that we are not aware of the problem ourselves. It is not a bad idea to have a good friend, spouse, or other relative whom you can trust tell you if you have any habits or problems of which you are not aware. Once you know about the problem, you can do something about it. Self-awareness will break bad habits or find a solution to a problem.

What is the purpose of all this? To make a favorable and lasting impression on those you meet, and to put you at ease—to give you poise. When you are able to motivate a favorable and lasting impression on others, that is when you are "accepted." And when you feel right, you automatically express that feeling with better posture and attitude. Good grooming has interesting by-products: Success shows in your facial expression and in your handshake, you command attention, and people are drawn to you. You motivate yourself toward being successful. When you look good, you feel good *and you act good!*

EIGHT
Develop a Magnetic Personality

Motivation makes others want to do something for you. A magnetic personality—that inward and invisible "appearance" you convey to others about yourself—can exert great power in making others want to act in your behalf.

PERSONALITY—
GENUINE OR COSMETIC?
In the eyes of others, your personality says something about you instantly. Right away people form an opinion as to whether you are genuine or make-believe, whether true or false. Even though a personality may at times be misread by others, eventually the real "you" will be apparent.

In many ways, personality may be thought of as the manner in which you communicate yourself to others. During courtship, a couple has no trouble making their feelings known to each other, even without words. A similar sort of communication is at work every time people interact with one another. We can tell from a person's personality if he or she is happy, and we know likewise if a person is depressed or worried; no one has to explain how that person feels; his or her personality communicates it to us.

THE ECHO-EFFECT OF MOTIVATION

Like attracts like. Opposites attract opposites. What these sentences are saying is that if you wish someone to like you, you have to like that other person. In other words, you receive exactly what you give away, what you impart to others. It is like an echo, like the words you have shouted to a mountain coming back to you in the same precise order. This is nothing new, the idea has been around since the beginning of time, and it has never been better expressed than in the Bible: "Whatsoever a man soweth, that shall he also reap."

There is a direct relationship here with what we have been saying about positive thinking and focusing and imaging. If we want something, we must think positively about it, we must focus on the end result of what we wish to accomplish. We must act accordingly. This makes our personality genuine. How could we attract a person to buy a product if we really did not want to make the sale? Our negative thought would discourage anyone from buying.

The "echo-effect" is a basic function of personality. The way we wish others to respond to us is the way we must express ourselves. There is no other way to be successful and to achieve happiness. Perhaps you have heard it said that a child becomes the manner in which he is treated: If he is treated with love, he becomes loving; if he is treated with meanness and ridicule, he becomes cruel and spiteful. To some extent, the same thing is true all our lives: We get from others as much as we give.

We need now to direct our attention to some of the ways the "echo-effect" can deliver for you.

WHAT DO PEOPLE WANT FROM YOU?

People who have no feeling for others, and who cannot learn to acquire it, are doomed to failure. They will be avoided. No one will come to their doors for help, and neither will they ever be successful in motivating others. Selfishness will be their mark.

A friend of mine was once offered a partnership in a marketing firm. He was flattered by the offer because the firm's head had done wonders for one company, really putting it on the map. But before reaching an agreement, my friend did some checking. He found that despite the early success he'd heard and read about, the marketing firm was losing customers right and left. Why? Because of the personality of the man who'd started the company. Deceived by early success, he believed he could do it all and, in the process, walked all over customers and employees alike. In fact, my friend could find no one in the industry who would speak well of the man. As a consequence, my friend turned down the offer. Several months later, he heard that two more disgruntled department heads had left the company. The president was left with virtually nobody, for he had no feeling for others and, as a result, had no one pulling for him to succeed. Spoiled by the first blush of success, he thought he could do it alone, but he couldn't.

If you want to be successful, you need the help of other people. You can get that support from them *only when you find what it is they want from you*. Furthermore, they will treat you the way you treat them. Your behavior will be reflected in their behavior.

What are some of the qualities of character that you wish for in others, which you therefore need to possess yourself?

MANNERS AND GRATITUDE

Gratitude must not be confused with good manners. We need to recognize the place of good manners in our society. Without them, there would be chaos. No doubt, the very origin of good manners was an attempt to be thoughtful of others. Eventually, however, the origin of manners became sunk in a mire of embellishments and protocol that obscured much of its purpose. And this lead to a social code that became the end-all of behavior. All meaning was lost. Thank-yous became mere words. Now we say thank you because it is considered good manners to say thank you. But gratitude is too often not expressed.

MOTIVATIONAL MEMO
There is no such thing as a self-made man. You will reach your goals only with the help of others.

People like to be thanked *genuinely* for what they do, and such is not an expression of ego; it is an indication that what they did was, in fact, something they should have done, something that was earned, something the other party recognized as an act of kindness and affection. A cold thank-you that conveys only good manners has little meaning—a mere nod to a social code of behavior. The response to kindness and affection is not a response to a social code; it is instead gratitude, which can be expressed in many ways.

There are few forces that break up friendships or that communicate lack of good personality more quickly than the absence of gratitude.

THE POWER OF HONESTY

A neighbor once remarked that she could tell if a person was honest, for honest people smile with their eyes rather than with their mouths.

If you haven't noticed a person smile, take time to do so. This neighbor was absolutely right; the place to look for honesty is in the eyes. We form our opinions of people by the way they react to others and by the way they communicate themselves to you; this is most frequently by way of the eyes.

The person who will not look you directly in the eye, who shifts his gaze from side to side, and who never smiles with his eyes, gives an impression of insincerity, of having no conviction, or of being untrustworthy.

You may lack certain abilities to do some of the things you would like to do, but honesty is a rubber stamp that can cancel your shortcomings and put you in direct communication with those you want to become close to.

Now, let's look at honesty as power. People become fearful when they have something to hide. The person who is honest has nothing to hide and as a result goes forth with strength and courage; his whole outlook and his appearance convey an appealing sense of integrity and respect. He is the kind of person with whom others want to be associated. He has power to motivate others in his direction.

FORGIVENESS

True forgiveness is the act of eliminating the past completely! Forgiveness is no good half-done. Unless forgiveness is absolute, there is no forgiveness.

It is much like coming into the house dirty and soiled after changing a tire. You go to the shower and the dirt and the grime are completely washed away down the drain out of sight forever. A sort of baptism—you become clean and others see you as clean.

Forgiveness works the same way. The trouble or irritation you were carrying around that another may have caused you has been completely washed away and forgotten forever if you truly forgive.

Researchers have proved that people who harbor grudges and bad feelings toward others, who cannot forget unpleasant happenings others caused them, can bring on themselves not only mental problems but also physical distress and illness. So, from a personal point of view, forgiveness is important. It restores a person to better mental and physical health.

It also restores friendship and contact with the person forgiven. Much as honesty shows in your eyes, so does your degree of empathy for another person, for in essence that feeling is an expression of honesty. Forgiveness, like honesty, is healing. It is an act of courage. It adds luster to your personality and motivates others to forgive you.

There are times, too, when you need to forgive yourself. How often have we been bothered by some unkindness we have done in the past and wished to forget? You can forget it. Forgive yourself and end all thoughts of it forever. Carrying around bitterness toward yourself for something done in the past can have the same consequences that resentment toward others can have—mental and physical consequences, a nervous breakdown or illness. Forgive yourself and believe that God will forgive you. Then go about your business as if the past had never happened.

HUMILITY
The personality is also magnetized by humility, and again this is a characteristic that attracts others to you and opens many doors. Any lack thereof is most obvious, for it becomes apparent in words and acts and with body and facial expressions. Unlike dirt, the absence of humility

can't be swept under the rug; it is there for all to see, and there is no covering it up. Humility admits mistakes, and it accepts criticism with kindness.

Humility also gives credit where credit is due. When the great running back O. J. Simpson was setting NFL rushing records at Buffalo, he was always careful to give credit to the linemen for blocking for him; he made it clear that he couldn't have done it without them. There is no limit to what can be accomplished if you don't care who gets the credit.

WIT AND HUMOR

How dull life would be if there were no wit and humor. How refreshing it is to hear a person tell a joke on himself, or to point out the humorous side of events.

Do you take life so seriously that you have no fun? If so, perhaps you are in the wrong business; maybe your goals should be changed. Goals should add zest and permit you to see the light side of life.

I have a strong urge to be with certain people just because they are fun. They draw others to them. They charge my batteries, so to speak; I derive energy from them. Conversely, I am not at all attracted to those who find no fun in life, who have nothing to offer but business, business, business.

Having fun and being funny are not the same. I enjoy people who are funny, but I also know people who try to be funny but somehow are not able to put it across. This person must be very careful that he or she does not unintentionally insult others. It is better to err on the downside than to go beyond one's abilities and hurt the feelings of others.

Regardless of whether you have wit and an ability to use it, your personality will motivate others in your direction if you will relax and not take life so seriously that you find no fun in it. Life is not meant to be boring; it is meant to be lived and to be full of expectation and excitement. Your personality should convey that outlook on life.

PERSONALITY AND LOVE

In the final analysis, a magnetic personality is one of love. Love embodies good character, gratitude, honesty, forgiveness, humility, and a sense of humor. Love is power and action. Love can open all doors, for it reproduces your love in others.

The best advice I can give about love is simple: If you love a person, tell him. So often we fail to do so, instead thinking the person knows it or doesn't need to hear it. After speaking to a convention, I was told by a top executive how touched he was by my topic of love.

He told me that his wife would from time to time suggest they go to lunch together. His reply was always the same: he'd like to, but he was just too busy.

On the morning of an important business meeting, his wife made the same suggestion: how about lunch? Again, the man begged off. Then during the meeting, he received word that his wife had been killed in an automobile accident. He commented, with tears in his eyes, that he would give up everything he had if somehow God would allow him to have his wife back for just one hour—to take her to lunch and to tell her he loved her.

The story is told that the beautiful singer and actress Mary Martin was about to go on stage for the premier of one of Oscar Hammerstein's musicals. A messenger delivered a note to Ms. Martin from Hammerstein, who was terminally ill with cancer. It read:

> A bell is not a bell 'til you ring it,
> A song is not a song 'til you sing it.
> Love in your heart is not put there
>   to stay;
> Love is not love 'til you give it away.

NINE
How to Build Successful Relationships

Life is an experience in relationships. Good relationships feature two healthy personalities, similar yet different. If you are going to build a good relationship, half of the relationship—your half—must be strong and adjusted.

SELF-WORTH
Self-worth is how you think and feel about your own self. Do you truly value and respect yourself?

Loving one's self is not egotism. It conveys no selfishness whatsoever. It is a recognition that you are a child of God, a unique and rare individual. Of all the people who have walked the earth since the beginning of time, there has never been another person like you, and there never will be. Think about that and realize how truly special you are. Remember, too, that

"God don't make no junk." Your abilities and talents, the potentials you possess, are not meant to lie dormant within you; they are meant to be expanded, to be shared with others, and to be used for good.

THE ART OF COMMUNICATING

When you and I talk, we hear words, but we also hear something more—*how* these words are spoken, the inflection of the voice. How I look when I talk to you, what you think of my appearance, my clothes, my voice and accent, these communicate something about me. And thoughts that I *do not* utter also say something to you about me. They are often more revealing than points I might try to make by punctuating my words with a pointed finger or by brushing a question aside with a smile or a smirk.

Our very being communicates so many things about us that unless we love ourselves and care for our own person, we cannot convey respect or communicate positively. How often we form an opinion of a person who may not even be speaking to us by the way that person acts. How we project and how we respond say more to others about ourselves than mere words could ever communicate.

Listening is also part of communicating. Do we really *hear* what others are saying to us, or do we form opinions only by their words? And when we listen, do we listen with respect or with ridicule? For others, like ourselves, are also unique and "not junk" in the eyes of God.

So, communicating is projecting ourselves into the mind's eye of another person. Listening is communication from another who projects into our mind's eye. The words may be beautiful, but they may be read in another way. Take for example the boy who was asked to spell and use the word *beautiful* in a sentence. His reply after spelling it correctly was, "When my brother came home last night and told Dad he'd wrecked the car, Dad said, 'Beautiful, just beautiful!'"

In nearly everything we do, we are communicating. A positive approach to self-worth will greatly enhance our success in the various relationship roles that make up life and that determine our success. Let's examine some of them.

Marriage. Marriage is one of the most serious commitments you can make. You are declaring your love for another person in front of the entire world. You ask the state to sanction your marriage, and you ask God to bless it. It requires both persons working full time to live up to this serious commitment. Love and cooperation must be freely given if marriage is to succeed; it cannot be an "I'll-do-this-if-you-do-that" kind of thing.

MOTIVATIONAL MEMO
Without real friends even a millionaire is poor. —*Forbes*

When you were first married, you probably experienced that wonderful, head-over-heels-in-love feeling from the very start. But sooner or later you probably encountered some conflict with your spouse over money, the children, or any of a number of other issues. To try to say in words that everything is all right when you are really communicating something else, belies your own feelings and disturbs the strong bonds that marriage requires. Marital conflicts and disagreements should be open affairs, with each partner stating in a frank and loving way what the problems are and trying to resolve them.

Working at a marriage takes time as well as commitment. If you permit outside activities or your work to have a higher priority than your marriage, the marriage will suffer. Marriage has to be nurtured, and time has to be found for nurturing it with the partner. A well-nurtured marriage relationship can handle the day-to-day problems and conflicts and strengthens the commitment that grows deeper each day.

Parenthood. From marriage we go to parenthood, where positive self-worth should be communicated to children.

So often we see families giving as much, or even more, in material goods to their children than budgets allow, at the same time neglecting their emotional support and security. Children have feelings of self-worth, and how their self-worth is nurtured by their parents can have a direct bearing on the child's development and on the child's outlook on life. Being a parent has responsibilities that require time and patience and demand dedication and love.

It is important to let children know you love them, to let them know your love is unconditional, that you will love them no matter what. This does not mean a child can do no wrong. You are doing your child no favor if you give him the message that whatever he does is right. You can disapprove of a child's behavior without disapproving of the child as a person.

Take pride in your children's accomplishments. Let them know you are proud of them. A child who has strong feelings of self-worth will later be able to cope with life's disappointments and setbacks. A child who has experienced little praise will usually fold under adversity.

Work Relationships. In business as in other relationships your feelings of self-worth affect your success. Whether you are an employee or an employer, you and those who work with you are bound together by a common goal: You both want the enterprise to succeed. You will do your best when you approach your job with self-confidence and an attitude of enthusiasm and cooperation. Let's take a look at some healthy attitudes about work.

A successful work relationship is based on mutual respect. As an employee, you recognize that your employer has given you certain responsibilities and duties to carry out in return for which you receive a salary; and, if you've found the job that's right for you, you receive a great deal of satisfaction.

As an employer, you respect your employees' abilities, you share responsibility, you make your expectations clear. You are open-minded, flexible, and work at creating an atmosphere of trust and goodwill. Your employees know they can talk to you, that their work is valued and respected. You show a genuine interest in their goals and aspirations.

The work relationship does not have to be friendship, although many a solid and longlasting friendship has started as a result of people working together.

Friendship. As important as a good marriage, home life, and a satisfying work situation are, we also need to reach outside those circles for friends.

An individual's success and an individual's self-worth can often be measured in terms of the number of friends he has. Friendship is a sharing of one's love of self with others. Without friendship, one is doomed to loneliness.

As a friend you expect to share your interests, enthusiasm, and troubles with others; you have common interests, whether they be jogging, gardening, reading books, a hobby, or a recreation. You are honest and open in your dealings. You value your friendship and tell your friends you appreciate them. You know your *friends can rely on you, and you know you can rely on them regardless of why or when.*

A friend is like an island of safety where you feel secure and where communicating is often without sound or motion. It's difficult to improve on George Eliot's definition of friendship: "Friendship is the inexpressible comfort of feeling safe with a person, having neither to weigh thoughts nor measure words."

SOCIAL LIVING

We are all part of humankind, and it is impossible to isolate ourselves. Whether at work or play, whether busy or waiting, whether at home or traveling, awake or asleep, well or ill, we constantly interact with others. Incidents thousands of miles away can change our lives so suddenly! Incidents close at hand can affect those who live thousands of miles from our shores. Individually and collectively, we are part of society.

Again, self-worth is not ego. Self-worth does tell us that we have an obligation to society and to the world at large. Paying taxes, voting, and defending our country are not by far the extent of our obligation. The hungry, the homeless, and the oppressed deserve our concern, our compassion, and our help. So do the problems waiting for answers to make life better for society as a whole.

The opportunities that await us are limitless and exciting, be they opportunities of family, of the work arena, or of the world. What we think of ourselves and how we go about spreading our own self-esteem determine how well these opportunities will be seized. Your attitude about yourself can be one of the strongest motivating influences in your life. You should not miss these opportunities. You won't if you take care to communicate your own self-worth and recognize the self-worth of others.

UNIT

III

OVERCOMING OBSTACLES

TEN
You Can Overcome Worry, Doubt, and Fear

Three of the worst mental enemies you have to conquer are worry, doubt, and fear. You face them daily. There is probably nothing else in life that can, if you let it, waste so much of your time and strength as do these three negative feelings. Yet, with the proper motivation you can conquer them. In fact, you must conquer them or else they will destroy your desire and ability to reach your goals.

DON'T BE A CHRONIC WORRIER

It is a rare person who does not experience worry, doubt, and fear during his life. It is a natural thing to do. But it is not natural when a person expresses such moods for no apparent reason or when he allows them to control his behavior.

There are many people who are chronic worriers, always uncertain about what is going to happen. As soon as one worry or doubt is dispelled, another takes its place. One suspects that perhaps these people would become extremely unhappy if they had nothing to worry about!

The chronic worrier fears it is too cold outside and he may catch infection if he goes out, or perhaps it is too hot and he will have a sunstroke. He may be fearful that someone will break into his house if he does not lock the doors and windows securely, and then fears he will be unable to escape if the house catches fire. Or his car will not make the turn if he speeds up; and if he doesn't speed up, the car behind may run him down.

Always unhappy. Always fearful. Always doubting a good outcome. A person to be pitied. It is hard for him to hold down a job and hard for others to be friendly and patient with him.

Then there is the person who worries because he believes his involvement in something gives him a legitimate reason for worrying. We do not categorize him as a chronic worrier although he may be.

He may be worried about things of the past. Did he do the assignment properly? Will he be punished or penalized for something he forgot to do? What were people saying behind his back? Will he be able to avoid someone whom he has offended?

And he may worry about the present. Is he doing his work the right way? Are people purposely avoiding him? Should he leave the key for his mother to get into the house? Is the slight congestion in his throat the beginning of cancer?

And what about the future? Will the seeds he planted really grow? Will the package he mailed reach the right person on time? Will it rain next Thursday when he has to go shopping? Will the plane crash on his trip to the coast next month?

We have pity for this person, too, for he is a timid soul, one who has little faith in his own abilities and one who lacks faith in God. How very unpleasant his life must be at times.

Does worry accomplish anything? There is the story of a farmer who had been prosperous all his life, in part because he'd worked hard, kept faith, taken each day as it came—and never worried. Yet all around him he saw people who worried about the weather, the state of the world, their health—you name it.

The farmer thought he might be missing something by not worrying, so he decided he would devote an entire day to worrying. He went to bed early, so he would be rested up for his day of worrying. The next morning he ate a big breakfast, figuring he would need lots of nourishment for a full day of worrying. Afterwards, he sat down in his favorite chair and commenced to worry.

He worried about what he'd do if his crops failed. He'd go broke. He worried about what he'd do if there was a bumper crop. That would drive prices down. He'd go broke. Then he worried about the state of his health. What if he got sick and couldn't work? He'd go broke. And what about the weather? If it didn't rain, there'd be a drought. No crops. He'd go broke. And if it rained too much? Why, the crops would wash away. He'd go broke. . . . The more he worried, the more the farmer found he had to worry about.

The next day, he saw his neighbor, told him what he'd done, and finished by saying, "Yep, twelve solid hours of worrying, and it *didn't accomplish a durn thing.*"

The farmer learned something we should all keep in mind: Worrying is unproductive. It never solved a single problem, and it never will. Only motivated positive action solves problems.

THE CAUSE OF WORRY, DOUBT, AND FEAR

Whether you are a chronic worrier or whether you express worry, doubt, and fear only occasionally, the cause is the same—fear of the unknown and not knowing how to react to it. You fear the situation will take you by surprise—something will happen suddenly. But what? And how will you react? Will you be able to handle it? What if you can't? Typically, this displays a combination of fear and lack of faith in yourself.

HOW TO OVERCOME WORRY, DOUBT, AND FEAR

It is possible to overcome these feelings—completely. But it demands motivation and action.

First, these concerns must be analyzed. They will fall into two groups—nonsubstantive concerns and those that have some basis of substance.

Whether the person is a chronic worrier or one who worries only from time to time, he must recognize that nonsubstantive concerns are those about which he can do nothing—absolutely nothing. This belief must be accepted completely. We have no control over next Thursday's weather, so it is ridiculous to spend any time worrying about it. Whether the seeds will come up or not and whether the package will arrive on time at its destination are matters no one can do anything about. Of course, you should give thought to how you'll react if it does rain on Thursday; you will need a raincoat or umbrella. And if you prepared the soil for your seeds, you did your duty. If you mailed the package in plenty of time and addressed it clearly, again, you acted responsibly. What happens from that point on is nothing you can control, and you are wasting your time being concerned about it.

So focus on being calm; think positively about what you have done. And if you have not acted responsibly, learn a lesson that you will not repeat.

Many people worry about health, fearing heart disease or cancer. This is another non-substantive concern. If you are taking proper care of your body and seeing your doctor regularly, what more can you do? If you use positive thinking, your life and your relationship with others can be happy. If you use negative thinking, you can lower your body's resistance to disease, become unhappy, and drag down those around you. The choice is up to you. The way you act will determine whether you subdue your concerns or fan them into even larger problems.

SUBSTANTIVE CONCERNS
But there are such things as substantive concerns—concerns for which there is a basis for being worried. We are not talking about imaginary troubles that occupy the chronic worrier, but rather about real ones that can involve anyone.

MOTIVATIONAL MEMO
Worry often gives a small thing a big shadow. —Swedish Proverb

These, too, should be categorized into types: those that concern the past and those that concern the present and future.

Type #1. Concerns involving the past. Again, there is probably little that can be done about a worry from the past. It has happened, and the lapsed time should be a healing period to allow you to banish the concern from your mind.

When Dr. Paul Brandwein, the famous science teacher, was on the faculty at George Washington High School in New York City, he used a simple yet dramatic demonstration to point out to his students how unproductive worry is. When the students would come into class, he'd have a bottle of milk perched on the laboratory desk. After they were seated and wondering what experiment the milk was for, Dr. Brandwein would startle the students by smashing the bottle of milk into the sink and exclaiming, "Don't cry over spilt milk."

He invited his students to gather around the sink. "Take a good look," he said, "because I want you to remember this lesson the rest of your lives. That milk is gone—you can see it's down the drain; and all the fussing and hair-pulling in the world won't bring back a single drop of it. All we can do is write it off, forget it, and go on to the next thing."

Sometimes we worry about past deeds we should not have done. Becoming angry and insulting a friend is a good example. The only way a situation like this can be completely remedied is to ask forgiveness from the person you insulted. Forgiveness has enormous healing powers that reinforce friendships with love and security.

Type #2. Concerns involving the present and future. These are concerns over which we have some control. Think of the sales rep who quoted the wrong discount to a customer and then had to make the sale based upon a larger discount than his company could afford. If it were an honest mistake, he should apologize to his boss and learn from this experience a lesson to be more careful in the future. A repeat of the incident could cost him his job, but the lesson, if applied in the future, could grant him greater job security. Dwelling on past mistakes is negative thinking; learning from them and avoiding making the same mistake twice is positive thinking.

We cause many of our worries, doubts, and fears because we neglect to analyze our own activities. There is the mother who worried that her child would not be promoted into the next grade because the girl had such a poor attendance record. She was always missing the school bus. The problem did not go away, and the school principal warned the parent what might happen if the child's attendance was not improved. The mother was so concerned about the problem that she did not see the solution. The solution was to wake the daughter a half hour earlier each morning and to assume some responsibility that she would make the bus on time.

How often we cause our own worries just because we fail to solve the situation that causes them. How often we raise doubts about our abilities just because we do not try to accomplish what we have been asked to do. How often we raise doubts about other people's motives that affect us just because we do not communicate with them and endeavor to make friends with them. Over and over it is lack of positive action on our part that causes us to fret and doubt. After all, it is we ourselves that make us what we are.

If we are concerned about the poison ivy in the yard, what have we done to get rid of it? If we are concerned about the speech we have to make, what have we done to prepare for it? If we are concerned about an overweight problem, have we done our best to restrict our diet, and have we been getting plenty of exercise? In all of these situations the solution requires self-motivated action. And once we have done our part, there is nothing more we can do about it. Worry, doubt, and fear are caused by people who do not work toward solutions. Instead, they live in fear that others will not solve their problems to their liking (which is probably correct).

TWO FACES OF FEAR

Fear is a powerful force that keeps millions of people from their accomplishments, and it can, in one way or another, prevent you from getting what you want in life. It is real. It stops people from taking advantage of an opportunity. It can tear you down physically, shorten your life, and actually make you ill. It can freeze you when you want to speak. I have seen opportunity pass right by people because they were afraid to act.

But fear should be looked upon squarely in its eye, for it is a healthy and natural thing to be afraid of certain things. Being afraid of death makes us drive cautiously. It is healthy to be concerned about your family, job, business, and future. These fears make you react in a positive way and are healthy ones. However, when you become afraid and worry about things beyond your control, then you are playing with trouble.

There are people everywhere who have conquered fear, people who are at ease everywhere and at all times. How do they do it? Through faith and action. Faith and action do cure fear. Faith in yourself, faith that you can work out your problems, and faith in God, knowing in your faith that God knows what is best for you and that, although you may not understand, he loves you and his plan for you will turn out best. Faith will always overcome fear. Psalm 34:4 says, "I sought the LORD, and he heard me, and delivered me from all my fears." It didn't say some of my fears, many of my fears, but *all of my fears.*

IMAGINED WORRIES

We have spoken about the chronic worrier. And we have said there are things he can do to overcome his problem.

But we should not forget that sometimes this person is in need of help from a professional counselor or from a doctor. If this is your problem, do not put off seeking help. For life, even with problems, can be beautiful, and professional help can assist you in making your life so. Life is action, and life is loving. Unless you can participate, you are doomed to unhappiness, and people will avoid you. But professional assistance will help to liberate you from your need.

Somewhere I saw a worry survey that says 40 percent of the things we worry about never happen, 30 percent are in the past and can't be helped, 12 percent concern the affairs of others that aren't our business, 10 percent are about sickness, either real or imagined, and only 8 percent are worth worrying about. I even question the 8 percent, for I know that with faith and action you can eliminate most of the worries, doubts, and fears that seek to prevent your happiness and the attainment of your goals.

ELEVEN
Master Your Tensions and Learn to Relax

It was recently brought to my attention that within the age group of men who are over fifty, at least 25 percent die from hypertension! I do not know the percentage for women, but it could well be approaching the percentage for men.

Imagine that—people dying, not from injuries, not from illness, but dying from the result of tensions. These are people who never learned to relax; instead they mischanneled their energies and destroyed themselves.

THE MANIFESTATIONS OF TENSION
There is a certain contagion about tension. For example, when you drive from a rural area on the outskirts of a large city such as New York, long before you reach the city there are noticeable signs of tension. Before crossing the

Tappan Zee Bridge, drivers are vying with one another for position on the thruway. Their driving can border on outright ruthlessness in many instances. They take advantages they would never take with a friend. Yet many of their highway targets could even be their friends, and there would be no difference. Their faces are without smiles and without warmth. In fact, a certain cruelty can be read in their faces. Anger mounts if they cannot pass, or if the car ahead is slow in leaving the toll booth. Their horns broadcast their impatience to surrounding cars and warn other drivers to beware. The closer you come to the city, the more you realize you have caught the rush fever; now you do to others what you, only a few minutes before, were criticizing other drivers for doing to you.

As you continue down the East or West Side drives, anger sets in, and you do your best to prevent the other drivers from merging in from the right. Perhaps by now your language is describing your thoughts, and you no longer apologize to your passengers for the words you use. The cab driver cutting in makes you angry toward all cab drivers, and you show outright contempt for the poor signals of the manager of the parking lot.

You hear the sound of the approaching subway and naturally join others running, pushing people aside, and jamming your way into an already overfilled subway car. You can't read your paper because of the crush; yet you will read it, and so will five others who are peeking over your shoulder. The elevator to your office is equally unfriendly and jammed, and you are in no condition to say good morning to anyone.

This is not the way you left the country. It was beautiful there when you left the farm. It is not beautiful here; you may even have learned now to hate the city. But you have work to do and people to see concerning your business. How pleased are others going to be to see you? Or have they also joined the pack?

WHAT CAUSES TENSIONS?

While the general name for all of this is tension, we have other names for the same thing: irritation, frustration, and nervousness.

But what is the cause of tension? Is it physical, or is it mental or emotional or what?

The main cause for tension in your life is that you have become out of balance in your living and work habits. You have forgotten yourself when you set the priorities for goals and for your work habits. *You have neglected to love yourself.* The center of your attention has been on busy work, the rat race, setting records, getting ahead, and the criteria the business world sets for success.

In the rush to meet these criteria, you have complicated your own problems. In order to break your record of prospects seen daily, you have not had time to answer your mail. You find it difficult to say no to additional requests for your time, and soon you do not have time to fulfill these commitments. Everything piles up. You feel yourself running against time. You feel like climbing a wall. There is no time for a rest or vacation. People with whom you work leave you alone because with all these pressures building up, your temperament has become edgy and abusive. Even your spouse and family complain. You gulp down your food to try to save time, forgetting completely how a colleague with the same habit ended up with a stomach ulcer. Round and round you go. There is no order to anything anymore, no time to visit the doctor for the annual physical examination, and no time for anything except hustle, bustle, and fretting.

Perhaps the above is an exaggeration so far as you are concerned; it is not, however, an exaggeration for many. It is a daily occurrence. And it describes the causes of many tensions, irritations, and frustrations. Depending on the individual case, these circumstances can break a person down physically. And if anger is a part of these tensions, the situation can become treacherous, both personally and interpersonally.

THE TYRANNY OF ANGER

Of all the emotions, the most harmful and insidious is, without any doubt, anger. Anger can be ruinous, destroying friendships, families, and personality. It also destroys business and health. But even worse, it is an indication you have lost control; your reasoning powers and logic have been destroyed. Problems that are "settled" in anger are never settled; there is always a remnant of hard feelings and guilt.

> **MOTIVATIONAL MEMO**
> You must be able to handle tension—not let it manhandle you. Relax! Calm down, stop rushing around, and take hold of your life.

Remember what the doctor told General Eisenhower after his first heart attack? Never allow yourself to become angry; it could be fatal!

"Count to ten before you allow yourself to become angry" is sound advice that has been passed down for many generations. Anger is a killer; it is behavior that results from negative thinking.

I would not try to argue that anger is not a natural reaction. It most certainly is. So is hunger, but we don't conquer hunger by staying hungry; we conquer hunger by killing the hunger pains. So when anger strikes, it must likewise be killed by doing something positive that will stop its growth.

One of the temptations of anger is to try to outdo one's adversary, to "get even." But no one "gets even." Anger begets anger, and in such instances withholding your anger while your adversary vents his will more often than not make him the fool and you the victor.

YOU CAN OVERCOME TENSIONS

Overcoming tensions is not at all impossible; in fact, it is rather easy to do. There are a number of specific things you can do to help.

First, you must find out why you have tensions. Finding out is half the cure!

Slow down and analyze your actions. You *must* slow down to do this, for part of the reason for your frustrations is that you are rushing around too much. Slow down and really analyze your activities. Make a list of all the things you are doing under pressure and endeavor to plan your activities on some sort of time schedule. Perhaps some activities should be dropped entirely if they are not producing good results for you. Perhaps several activities should be combined. Perhaps a new activity should be substituted for one or more of your present ones.

But there is something equally important that you must do, and that is to calm yourself.

Your strength is in "quietness and confidence," as Isaiah the prophet wrote. How do you get this quietness and confidence? First, you have to want them. You have to be motivated.

There are many ways to quiet a person in order to give him or her confidence and energy. Let us look at some of them.

The therapeutic value of music is well known. You can feel the tension roll away as you sit at the piano and play something soft, or even bang on the keyboard to release the frustration you feel. If you don't play an instrument, you can enjoy music through listening.

The miracles of nature must have been designed for the same purpose. Sunsets, sunrises, cloud formations that silently shift from one design to another, the songs of birds, the faces and fragrance of flowers, the various colors of foliage—all these and more have a subduing effect upon the one who is nervous and high-strung. "Then there is always the garden," as a verse goes, and how helpful flower and vegetable gardens have been to ease one's mind and slow down the pace. It is miraculous how quickly a garden can make one forget the cares of the day. Spending time with children has this same calming effect for many who find themselves deeply immersed in the activities of small ones. Various sports, such as jogging, swimming, and bicycling, release tensions and at the same time have additional health benefits. Hobbies and pets and travel pay big dividends in the wonders they perform to slow a person down.

There are several forms of meditation that have shown remarkable ability in helping to overcome personal stress. Simple meditation is practiced daily by many—even by businessmen in their offices for a few minutes several times a day. This is a system that has been used by Orientals for ages and ages, and only recently has the Western world wakened to its benefits.

But perhaps the greatest way to relax is to observe regular private periods of prayer. In both the Old and New Testaments, people have been exhorted to prayer and reflection to calm their fast-paced bodies and minds. "Be still, and know that I am God," is a beautiful line from Psalm 46. Psalm 121 is an inspiring song assuring safety and help to those who look to God for help. And the first verse of Proverbs 15 is the promise that "a soft answer turneth away wrath." These are but a sprinkling of Bible references that caution one to slow down, to be quiet, and to find strength to replace tensions, nervousness, and frustration.

These private and quiet times also present an opportunity to observe your own behavior. How orderly are you about your work and other activities? Do you purposely put things off until you are hard against a deadline that is impossible to meet? Are you orderly in what you do, or do you create work and problems that have to be cleaned up after you are through? Meditation and other quiet times are designed for you to take a close look at yourself and come up with ways to eliminate the clutter you may have been accumulating—a time to make resolutions to do better. They should not be once-a-month periods of meditation and positive relaxation; they should be practiced without fail each day.

STOP AND ACT

We often hear that people get into trouble and generate tensions when they have nothing to do. I certainly do not disagree with that. Action is the one thing that in the final analysis will overcome tension. But it has to be positive action—action that is orderly and meaningful, action that is efficient and purposeful. And this type of action comes only after one has gone into a private session with himself through prayer, meditation, or some other means to gain calmness and establish a situation in which he can plan his actions. "Stop and act" sounds incongruous at first, but action without first stopping serves only to create the situation one is trying to avoid.

Earlier we discussed loving oneself and how

important that is. Ridding everyday living of tensions and frustrations must have a high priority for all who believe that loving oneself is important. It is also a first step toward loving others.

TWELVE
You Can Overcome Failure

It's not whether you get knocked down.
It's whether you get up again.
—Vince Lombardi

Have you ever failed?

Of course you have. We all have. But, as Vince Lombardi's quote implies, failure is only final if you let it be.

SOME VIEWS OF FAILURE

I have heard some contradictory ideas about failure. One goes like this: We forget our successes and remember our failures. The other idea is that we forget our failures and remember our successes. I suspect the truth is this: The first idea describes a human tendency, while the second tells us what we ought to do.

We *do* sometimes brood about our failures, replaying them endlessly in our heads, trying to figure out what went wrong. However, we *should* take pride in what we have accomplished; we should remember our successes and try to build on them.

Rich DeVos and Jay VanAndel, cofounders of the fabulous Amway empire, have a perceptive view of failure. VanAndel calls it "a marvelous word." DeVos agrees: "One of the best in the English language."

Why? VanAndel again: "Failure is the bridge. Sure, some people stop in the middle of it and jump off, but others recognize that the bridge has a brand new plot of land at the other end. Just keep on walking. And don't be afraid if you find yourself on another bridge someday—and another, and another. They all lead somewhere. The idea is not to stop walking, and most important, to know where it is that you want to go."

DeVos and VanAndel know what they're talking about. Together, they've crossed many bridges.

FAILURE IN PERSPECTIVE

But building on our successes while ignoring our failures is not all there is to it. We can also *learn from our failures.* We can examine how and why we failed, what we did wrong, how we can do better next time. Then—and only then—after we have learned all we can from our mistakes, should we forget them.

A story about Bart Starr and Vince Lombardi of the Green Bay Packers illustrates the point: Late in a game the Packers were winning; Starr dropped back to pass. Under a heavy rush, he threw in a hurry, and the ball was intercepted. Green Bay lost the game. Afterwards, Lombardi chewed Starr out in front of the entire team. Nobody on the team felt worse than Starr. He knew he should have "eaten" the ball and been thrown for a loss rather than risk interception. But later, Lombardi came to Starr and told him that now that he'd learned from his mistake, he ought to forget it completely.

That's how it should be with your failures. You feel bad about them, you wish they hadn't happened, but they did. Nothing in the world can change that. But you can change your attitude toward your failures. Like Starr, you can learn from the failure and then forget it.

WHAT FAILURE MEANS
Here are five things about failure you should remember:

1. *To fail is not to be a failure.* Your failure merely proves that you are human. It also says some-

thing good about you: that you tried. To try to accomplish anything, to *be* anything, is to risk failure. To completely avoid failing is to attempt nothing, to *be* nothing.

2. *Once you've learned from your failures, forget them.* I've said this before, but it's worth repeating. If you brood about your failures, you'll soon see nothing else. As a human being, you have something about you that is successful. Concentrate on that. Build on your successes, but learn from your failures.

You've heard this expression: Nobody's perfect. And it's true. Nobody is. And you're no exception. Why should you be? Failure is no disgrace. If it were, we'd all be pretty disgraceful people, wouldn't we? For, the truth is, we've all had our share of failures.

3. *You're never a failure as long as you keep trying.* Failure is no disgrace when you've tried your best. It *is* disgrace to live without goals, without challenges, and without taking risks. Without goals we have nothing to strive for, nothing to force us to grow and become more than we are. Better to fail attempting great deeds than to attempt nothing and succeed.

4. *Failure is never final—unless you let it be.* The fact that you have failed in the past, or are

failing now, is no reason to believe you will continue to fail. If you've read my first book, you'll know that I failed so many times in my efforts to establish a business that I finally found myself on the verge of bankruptcy. In fact, I was advised by some experts to give up and file for bankruptcy.

But I didn't. Now, there are a lot of people who helped me to achieve success in business. I also believe that God had a whole lot to do with it. Still, the choice was there: play it safe or get up and fight one more round.

The message is this: You are never a failure until you give up and quit trying. We learn from our failures how *not* to do things. Edison failed at his first six thousand attempts to develop a light bulb. When asked if he was discouraged, he replied: "No. I am now well informed on six thousand ways you cannot do it." Like Edison, we sometimes need to learn failure before we can learn success.

The greatest failure in life is to stop trying.

PEOPLE WHO BEAT FAILURE

Sometimes when others give us little chance to succeed, we must have confidence in our own ability and keep working toward our goals.

Harold Russell, a sergeant paratrooper, lost his hands in an accident. He was overwhelmed by a sense of failure and defeat. He was terrified to go through life without his hands. He didn't much care whether he lived or died. Then one day another soldier who lost his hands visited Russell in the hospital. He told him that the first and greatest obstacle he had to overcome was himself. The old soldier then quoted these words from Emerson: "For everything you have missed, you have gained something else." The loss of his hands was the turning point of his life. He became a best-selling author, married his childhood sweetheart, and achieved success and happiness beyond the dreams of most men.

Joseph Sorrentino started life on the mean streets of a tough Brooklyn neighborhood. A high-school dropout, he'd been in a hundred gang fights and given a dishonorable discharge from the Marine Corps for a bad attitude and fighting—all by age twenty.

After the marines, Sorrentino went back to the streets, hanging out with the Condors, his gang. His idol was an older boy. Sorrentino recalls, "I wanted to be just like him. He was tough, and he knew a lot about getting money the easy way. But one night while we were out on a rumble, I saw my hero's head blown off. I had to identify the body for the police, and I suddenly realized something had changed my life.

"Up to then I thought we Condors were

comic book characters, especially when the papers wrote us up after one of our rumbles. We all thought we were sort of young Supermen. But when I looked down at the body of my hero, I knew none of us were comic book heroes. We were real people, and one of us wasn't alive anymore."

Sorrentino says he realized then "that if I kept on as I was, it wouldn't be long before I would be lying in the street like my friend. So I made up my mind that I wouldn't let that happen to me."

But Sorrentino had a long way to go. Remembering the words of a high-school teacher, Mrs. Lawson, who had told him he could be a good student if he tried, he decided to go back to school, first making up in night school the three years of high school he had missed. During the day, he earned the money to support himself by plucking chickens.

After getting his high-school diploma, Sorrentino wanted to get as far away from his old environment as possible, so he enrolled at UCLA. After struggling through his freshman year, he got a scholarship.

By his junior year, Sorrentino, who'd been so busy studying he didn't have time for anything else, began to blossom in other ways: He won a weight lifting contest, became a wrestling champ, and played intramural football. His senior year, he was elected student body president and graduated *magna cum laude*. After graduation, Sorrentino could have taken the rewards for his hard work and accepted a good position with a number of companies. Instead, "I went back into the marines. I wanted to go back and right a wrong. I felt I had left a bad mark and wanted to change it to a better one. So I put in a year of active service and two years of inactive, and I got an honorable discharge."

Joe's next giant step on the way up from the streets was Harvard law school, another big adjustment. "The Radcliffe girls I tried to date didn't believe I was a law student. I still had the speech and mannerisms of a street person. They thought I was part of the Harvard maintenance crew.

MOTIVATIONAL MEMO

Many people consider themselves failures because they failed some subjects in school, or failed to make the team, or failed to make the club, etc. Failing means you were not as prepared as you could have been—but keep trying because you are never a failure until you completely give up.

"But I kept on working on my vocabulary [which he'd started to do as a speech major at UCLA] and after three years, I won the school's forensics competition. Then—it was hard for me to believe—I was selected class valedictorian."

As valedictorian, Sorrentino gave the commencement address. *Time* magazine saw fit to reprint it on a full page. That speech included the following thoughts:

> There are certain qualities in human beings that cannot be measured by aptitude tests, such as courage, drive, determination, and creativity. No matter what you are told negatively on a scale of measurement, you should not become discouraged. Low estimates cannot dim the flame of high aspiration. A test result can be a very unromantic decree. It can tell a person at a young age that he can't be anything. I knew that was not necessarily how it had to be. It could have been for me, but I had made up my mind not to let it. I had seen how life could have ended—on a street or in the county morgue.

Joe Sorrentino, a dead-end kid from the streets of Brooklyn, became a juvenile court judge in Los Angeles County.

Ann Person is another person who just refused to quit.

First, the little grocery store she and her husband ran in a small Oregon town began to fail. Herbert, her husband, turned to logging to supplement their income until he broke his back in a logging accident. The business collapsed.

They were compelled to sell vitamins door-to-door. The aircraft dealership they invested in "never got off the ground." Ann began selling picture frames and printing, and taught sewing.

Five years after her husband's accident, Ann was in a car accident and was an invalid for two years.

The accident forced Ann to concentrate on her favorite activity—sewing. She gave classes and because of her experience, created a basic technique and special pattern-to-sew kits. Days, she taught her new method throughout Oregon. Nights, she worked, cutting new patterns out of butcher paper.

Her first Stretch-and-Sew fabric center, offering classes and fabrics to customers, opened in Burns, Oregon, in 1967. Now there are 210 franchise and company-owned stores throughout the U.S. and Canada doing $74 million a year!

Failure, even tragedy, didn't stop Ann Person from trying. Through her ingenuity and perseverance she became successful.

MORE WAYS TO BEAT FAILURE
When day-to-day problems become discouraging, remind yourself of the many

successful people who overcame personal handicaps. Gene Littler overcame cancer to make a great comeback in golf. Norman Vincent Peale was extremely shy as a young man, but he became one of the world's most respected religious leaders. Helen Keller was born blind and deaf but became a great writer. O. J. Simpson was called "Straw Legs" when he was a boy because his skinny legs were crippled by rickets. Yet he became the greatest running back in the history of professional football.

These are people you've heard of. But there are many others whose stories of conquering failure are just as inspiring and exciting. We are apt to overlook the person next door who became a doctor, but not until he had spent four extra years in school because he had to work to pay his bills. Or the young widow with four children to raise, four children who became professional leaders. Or the girl who was born without hands and became a brilliant and well-known artist, holding the brush in her teeth. There are unsung heroes all around us, people just like you, who have looked failure straight in the eye and beaten it.

All these people, the great and the lesser known, who have overcome failure or who have avoided failure that was waiting for them, have had many common qualities.

—They used failure as a challenge, as a learning experience, and as a stepping-stone to success.

—They focused on success. They saw themselves achieving their goals.

—Despite failure, they kept at it—hard work, patience, and determination finally paid off.

—They had persistence and faith.

Teddy Roosevelt's words are just as true today as when he said them:

It's not the critic who counts, not the man who points out how the strong man stumbled or where the doer of deeds could have done better. The credit belongs to the man who is actually in the arena, whose face is maned by dust and sweat and blood; who strives valiantly; who errs and comes up short again and again, who knows the great enthusiasms, the great devotions, and spends himself in a worthy cause; who, at the best, knows in the end the triumph of high achievement; and who, at the worst, if he fails, at least fails while daring greatly, so that his place shall never be with those cold and timid souls who know neither victory nor defeat.

THIRTEEN
Learn from Your Mistakes and Struggles

Abundant life is a direct result of struggle. Show me a person who is willing to struggle in this great game called life, and I will show you a person heading for victory.

It is wrong for people to equate mistakes with failure, yet that happens frequently. Also, struggling to avoid mistakes and struggles are valuable learning experiences. I know I have gained a great deal from mistakes and struggles in my life.

LOOK TO NATURE
If you know where there is a bird's nest, keep track of it until the birds hatch. Sometime thereafter the mother bird will know when it is time for her young to spread their wings and leave their nest for good. She knows they are strong enough to fly. But watch them. Some are timid

and dare not leave the security of their nest. Others don't quite make up their minds. Soon the mother bird will stop coaxing them and actually push them out of the nest, for she knows they have the strength to fly if they want to. But look under the nest a day or two afterward. Sometimes you will find a dead bird or two— birds that just dropped to the ground without a struggle, birds that were too timid to struggle or even to try to fly. Their unwillingness to struggle was their mistake. Now they are dead. Those that struggled are alive.

Take a look at trees growing on barren soil. Some of our most beautiful trees grow on mountainsides where there is deep rock and inadequate surface moisture for normal growth. Here you find two kinds of trees— those that have struggled and sent forth their roots far below, deep between the rocks and into crevasses, to find water and soil substance, and those that have given up the struggle and died.

Over and over in nature we find the same type of thing happening. From common stock, there are offspring that have to struggle to succeed and others that die for lack of struggle. And there must be some lesson to all this. Indeed, there is. Life is a struggle, a constant struggle. And where there is not struggle, there is no life—only death.

THE ELEMENTS OF
GROWTH AND CHANGE

So there is no life where there is no struggle, and neither is there struggle where there is no change. Struggle is never stationary; it is always in the direction of change. The opposite of change is death.

From the beginning of our lives we struggle to do something that results in change, for change is growth. We change from the young child who partially takes care of himself, to the young person who goes to school and seeks guidance from his elders, to the mature person who must earn a living for himself and his family, to the older person whose activities are eventually slowed until he can change no more. From birth to death, life is a struggle, a learning process. During this learning process, we borrow for our own use those things, material and nonmaterial, that our predecessors have discovered and learned; and during the days of our lives we press forward to discover new things that we will pass on to those who follow us. That is change, that is growth, that is struggle.

Growth and change are the sources of new opportunities. When we outgrow a pair of shoes, we get a brand new pair. When we outgrow a dress or a suit, we purchase a new one. And when we get no more use from an idea, growth and change assist us in finding new ones. Struggling shows you powers you never knew you had and never would have discovered without struggling. This constant change from one thing to another is the result of struggle, the result of growth.

MISTAKES IN THE HIERARCHY OF SUCCESS

An examination on which a student answers all questions correctly does not tell you what the student does not know. It tells you only that the questions he answered were ones he knew. But since no one knows everything about anything, how does one find out what the student does not know? By asking him more questions, by probing beyond the questions he answered correctly. Only when the student encounters questions for which he does not have the answers does one determine the limits of the student's knowledge and ability.

Try to imagine a mathematics student knowing all the answers to everything pertaining to his subject. Impossible, you say, and impossible would be right. First, the student learns some fundamentals of mathematics; he never starts the second year of mathematics without mastering the first year. He is tested on the principles until he has mastered them; then he advances to the next level of learning. But if he fails on the first level, he has to repeat it successfully before he can approach the next level.

There is a hierarchy to successful learning. It is first to learn the fundamentals, to make mistakes, to locate what you do not know, and then to advance to the next step.

So, mistakes are useful; they are milestones on the road to learning; they are guides to what you have missed. There is nothing wrong with mistakes at all. They are not indications of failure, but rather indications that you have not grasped something basic or that the person instructing you has not presented the material properly and in an orderly manner.

Everyone who grows makes mistakes. *You learn from mistakes; the real error is to stop trying.*

Think for a moment of the researchers who spent years and years trying to find a solution to polio, or to measles, or to smallpox. With each "mistake" they were able to eliminate one factor and zero in on something new. Eventually, they discovered prevention for these diseases. But if they had not been allowed to make mistakes, we would have no way to counter these dread diseases today.

Mistakes are indeed a part of the learning process—a most valuable part. And they must be recognized as a valuable part. Mistakes enable you to focus on the solution, to take forward steps in the direction of an answer you want.

We need to be allowed to make mistakes. They are indeed important in the hierarchy of success.

Oliver Wendell Holmes once said, "If I had a formula for bypassing trouble, I wouldn't pass it around. Wouldn't be doing anybody a favor. Trouble creates a capacity to handle it. I don't say embrace trouble. That's as bad as treating it as an enemy. But I do say meet it as a friend, for you'll see a lot of it and better be on speaking terms with it."

THE ANATOMY OF FAILURE

I would not want anybody to believe there is no such thing as failure, for there certainly is.

But failure is a state of mind, a negative state of mind, a state in which one believes there is no good, no progress, nothing to be learned. It is at the very opposite end from positive thinking, goals, and motivation.

The bird that was pushed out of the nest and would not even try to fly failed. The trees that did not put down their roots to find food and water failed. When we are overcome with our mistakes and will learn nothing from them to help us on the road to success, we fail. There is no growth and no change.

MOTIVATIONAL MEMO
Success isn't the opposite of failing. A runner may come in last, but if he beats his

best record, he succeeds. —Robert
Schuller

Most baseball fans have heard of Ty Cobb, one of the game's greatest players. During his remarkable career he stole more bases than anyone else and set a record that stood until just recently. But did you know that there was a player who was a *better* base stealer than Ty Cobb?

His name? Max Carey. One season he attempted fifty-three stolen bases and succeeded fifty-one times—an unbelievable 96 percent. Ty Cobb stole ninety-six bases the year he set the record. But he tried 134 times. That's only 71 percent. Yet, because he was willing to try harder and chance failure, he became one of the legendary names in baseball. Max Carey, who played it safe, is not remembered.

Like Ty Cobb, you're going to make mistakes. But keep trying. If you win often enough, people will soon forget the times you failed.

It has always bothered me that we say a student has "failed" if he has to repeat a subject or if he has to repeat a grade in school. He may have made mistakes and been unable to catch up with his fellow classmates, but he has not failed unless he has given up for good, quits school, and will not use his mistakes to overcome the "failure" grade given to him by his teacher. History has far too many names of men and women it calls successful who at one time or another had to repeat a course or a grade in school. And very frequently the reason a person is unable to master the subject matter of his course the first time is no fault of his but rather the inability of his teacher to inspire him. We do not have to look far to see the difference between good and poor teachers. This difference is no reason to blame the student for his inability to master a course. But this difference is a challenge for all teachers to master the skills of good teaching or else leave the profession to those who are able to inspire their students.

Fear of failing is another reason for failure. In this instance the person himself is largely responsible for failure. Recently a well-known concert pianist was asked what is the most difficult thing about memorizing music. "Fear," she said, "fear that you will forget." And she went on to describe how students who fear they will forget the music will do so almost as if on cue when they come to a point in the composition they were fearful about.

So, in summary, failure is negative thinking, the decision to do nothing about the mistakes and problems one faces as things change and as one grows. Learning from mistakes and struggling to overcome these mistakes are a learning process, positive thinking, goal-orientation, a sign of growth.

THE ANATOMY OF GROWTH

When we watch a seedling or a small child grow, it is easy to believe that there is very steady growth from birth to maturity. In just a few months the plant will mature and bear fruit. In just a few years the child will grow and mature into adulthood.

But the process of learning is somewhat different from that of the plant and the child. There are plateaus we achieve, leveling out sometimes for long periods of time before sending our learning curve upward again. Sometimes the curve even dips downward for a while, and it will continue downward if we let discouragement and lack of self-motivation rule our lives. When we tend to become discouraged, we must look at the main thrust of the curve. If it is generally upward, despite some plateaus and some downward bends, it is a normal growth curve, and there is no need for discouragement.

There is another difference between man's learning curve and the comparison with plants and the growth of the small child. Plants and small children very often depend on other factors outside of themselves for the fast growth they seem to exhibit. For instance, plants have to be weeded to prevent their being choked, they have to be watered and pruned, and they have to be guarded against destruction by insects. And the small child has to be fed and nourished by his mother while he is growing and learning to do these things for himself.

While we do depend on outside factors to aid our learning process, we are much more responsible to ourselves to reach new heights. And it becomes very important that we exercise control over our learning habits, that we do become responsible for our learning behavior.

Failure to do so is well illustrated by an incident that happened in the West Coast town of Monterey some years ago. Monterey used to be a California paradise for pelicans. After fishermen cleaned their fish, they would throw the entrails to the pelicans. The birds would become content, fat, and lazy. Eventually, ways were discovered to make use of the entrails commercially, and the pelicans were out of free meals.

The pelicans made no effort to fish for themselves. They would not struggle for food; they just waited around and became thin and weak. Many starved to death. They had forgotten how to fish for themselves.

Growth requires that we be responsible and that we be independent. We are not children who are tended by loving parents, but mature adults who are in charge of ourselves.

Growth then is work, doing something, action with a positive inspiration. And that is what struggling is—work. Struggling has a definite and useful purpose. Struggling forces you to develop your mental and physical abilities, to arouse your enthusiasm, to inspire your imagination, and to build your faith. Struggling also keeps you from becoming lazy and forces you to fulfill your mission in life.

Do not be afraid to make mistakes. You *will* make them. Gain from your errors. Don't repeat them. The mistake is to stop trying. You must *experience!* I can tell you, motivate you, guide you, but *you* must take action. Actions have a greater influence than words. You need to participate in life. You need to be willing to struggle, and you must prepare to be ready when the opportunity comes. You will not be judged by what you start, only by what you finish.

> If you won't change, you are dead.
> If you won't grow, you are dead.
> It's up to you!

FOURTEEN
Solve Your Problems

I accept problems as challenges. Why?

Problems are the very essence of maturing and the very essence of motivation. When there are no problems to solve, I know there is no progress. It is time to investigate, for lack of problems is a big problem in itself.

Why do I view problems as opportunities? Because problems give me an opportunity to put to work those things which I believe in: goals, focusing, positive thinking, faith in God, faith in others, faith in myself, love of family, and those with whom I work. I do not look upon problems as a testing period but as a challenge, an opportunity to use my talents for the betterment of others and to improve myself and my business. Problems make us bigger, and as we become bigger, we get bigger problems.

I honestly believe all problems are solvable. This doesn't mean that I will solve all my problems, but I do believe that each problem has its potential solution. I'll work to solve as many problems as I can.

Where would we be today if there had been no problems to be solved? We would have no stoves if there had been no problem of keeping warm, no cars if there had been no problem of getting somewhere quickly, no milk and food for the needy if there had been no problem about transporting it fresh before it spoiled, no cure for scurvy and polio if there had not been a problem of people dying and being left deformed from these dread diseases, and no homes if there had been no problem of shelter.

Problems can change the destiny of individuals and corporations. An example? A forgetful worker at a small soap factory in Cincinnati forgot to turn off his machine while he went to lunch. The result? A frothing mass of lather filled with air bubbles. He almost threw it away, but it was made into soap anyway. The soap floated. The citizens of Cincinnati could find it easily when they bathed in the waters of the Ohio River.

Thus was born Ivory soap, a mainstay of Proctor and Gamble. And it couldn't have come at a better time. In that year of 1879, Proctor and Gamble's main product up to that time—candles—were about to be superseded by Thomas Edison's light bulb!

So often problems create opportunity. During the summer of 1918 a young man from Utah visited Washington, D.C. He found the stifling heat and humidity very oppressive. No weather like that in Utah.

Years later, remembering that muggy weather, he bought the A & W Root Beer franchise for the nation's capital. He opened his stand in the summer of 1927, and business was terrific. Customers loved the cold root beer served in frosty mugs.

But by November, the chilly winds of winter quenched Washingtonians' thirst for the ice-cold beverage.

No customers is a fatal problem for any business. The owner could've closed up shop. But instead, he turned the problem into an opportunity. How? He changed the name of his stand to the Hot Shoppe and served chili, hot tamales, coffee, and sandwiches.

Fifty years later, that owner, John Willard Marriott, presides over an empire that includes 450 restaurants, 34 hotels, and cruise ships.

Today we are faced with some of the most terrifying problems the world has ever had to face: threats of war, the problem of starvation in many parts of the world, the problem of crime at home and abroad, the problem of poverty, of energy shortage, of race hatred, of nuclear waste, and many other troubles that face the nations of the world.

But am I still optimistic that they can be solved? Indeed I am. I still believe there is a solution for every problem, and whether the problem is one that confronts me personally or one that confronts society, I shall do my utmost to help solve that problem, knowing that I shall be successful with many of them.

HOW TO SOLVE PROBLEMS
I believe there are six steps to solving problems, and the solution to any problem should involve all six:

1. Don't fear the problem—calm down.
2. Study the problem but don't clutter your mind with it.
3. Concentrate on the solution, even a simple one.
4. Proceed from the known to the unknown.
5. Select a solution that is good for others as well as for yourself.
6. Act, even when a little risk is necessary.

By the way, there are no good shortcuts. While you may be successful occasionally in skipping a step, you do so at your own risk.

Shortcuts are great timesavers sometimes, but not when you are trying to solve problems. And the reason is that any problem being solved requires a proper state of mind and a logical attack. If you are not ready mentally to analyze the problem, you are defeating yourself by trying to do so. Furthermore, if you do not attack the problem logically, you are not going to find a logical solution.

Don't Fear the Problem. Fear is negative thinking. Negative thinking is no way to try to solve a problem. The mind must be cleared of negative thoughts. A cool mind thinks better than a worried mind. It must not feel it is under penalty or punishment because the problem has arisen. It must feel receptive and confident to be able to tackle a problem—confident that a solution is possible. Only then will you be able to use your hidden talents to assist in finding a solution to your problem. Approach a problem with enthusiasm and excitement, just as you would with something new that demands your attention. Only then will you be able to focus on the analysis and solution of your problem.

Study the Problem. Study and analyze the problem. Break it into parts if necessary. Talk to your associates and friends who understand the problem. Get their advice. Try to determine how it came about, what the sequence of events was that lead up to it. Who was involved and in what way? What warnings of its appearance did you receive? Get all the facts you can muster concerning the problem, *and get the right facts*. Forget your hunches as to why the problem occurred; just think of the facts of the case. Analyze the problem until you know as much about it as possible. Know which factors were controllable and which were not. Maintain faith that a solution, and a proper one, is possible.

Concentrate on the Solution. Now that you have analyzed the problem so you have all the information about its occurrence, the reason it happened and why, you should no longer concentrate on the problem. Put the problem into your subconscious. Now you should direct all your thoughts toward the solution. I cannot emphasize too much how important it is to keep the thought of a solution foremost in mind. Far too many people dwell on the problem over and over, giving little or no thought to the solution. Soon they start blaming themselves or even others for the problem. This makes matters worse, and the idea of a solution fades farther and farther away. Start concentrating on a solution, putting the various pieces together into a plan that will exorcise the problem or prevent its ever happening again. Determine what it is you wish to accomplish, how soon, who will be involved, and all the other principal parts of the plan; but don't get mired in details—they can be worked out after the solution has been arrived at. And don't become bogged down in your own likes and dislikes—keep them out of it.

It is a common fault to believe that big problems require big solutions. Keep them simple. Many of the biggest problems are cured by simple solutions. Don't overreact. Don't try to predetermine a solution; let the solution work itself out after you have analyzed the problem. There may be more than one solution—pick one and don't waste time.

And do not become discouraged. If you succeed once in one hundred tries you have succeeded!

PROCEED FROM THE KNOWN TO THE UNKNOWN

One mistake people often make when faced with difficulties is to strike off in different directions for a solution without first taking into consideration knowledge they already possess that may help them in reaching a clear-cut solution. From one's analysis of a problem, one should discover facts that will assist in looking for a solution. For instance, if a problem arises that has some of the same ingredients as a former problem had and you have learned from your past experience that certain things should or should not be repeated, why not use this practical knowledge to build your solution on? Go from the known to the unknown. If a certain type of action was not successful for a specific product, determine whether it could be used on a new product—but don't hazard wild guesses when it is possible to go from the known to the unknown.

MOTIVATIONAL MEMO
The motivated person views problems as challenges: You'll be successful if you allow problems to motivate you to find simple productive solutions.

Select a Solution That Is Good for Others as Well as for Yourself. One of the great service organizations of the world, Rotary International, has what it calls a Four-Way Test of the things we think, say, or do. This Four-Way Test provides just the right ingredients for the right kind of solution we are looking for:

Is it the *truth?*

Is it *fair* to all concerned?

Will it build *good will* and *better friendships?*

Will it be *beneficial* to all concerned?

It is a rare problem that concerns only one individual. The fact that more than one person is concerned is usually the reason the problem exists in the first place. A unilateral, one-sided, or selfish solution will solve no problem whatsoever; it will only prolong and increase the intensity of it.

Act on Your Solution! Over and over in these chapters, I have admonished you to act. Again, when you have a solution, it does no good to sit on it. It requires action—your action. And the sooner you can act, the quicker the problem will be solved.

There are those who believe that problems solve themselves, and they just tuck them away, hoping that time will dispose of them. Actually, this cannot happen if we apply the Four-Way Test, for others who are part of the problem are inconvenienced, and secondary problems are almost always generated until the prime problem is eventually solved. In the meantime, the person who shirks his duty and hopes that time will solve his problem loses the respect of his colleagues and shows up being the poor manager that he is.

When to act is another matter. It is not necessary to wait until you are 100 percent dead certain of the solution. You can act when there is some risk involved, providing you have reason to believe in the risk you are taking. If you are walking a nature trail and up ahead you see a large rock and behind it you see 90 percent of a bear, you don't have to see 100 percent of it before you decide to seek shelter. The same is true with action; don't put off implementing the solution even though you don't have 100 percent of the solution worked out. If you have worked on the solution in a composed and confident way, you should have the wisdom and knowledge to implement it before you have all the details worked out.

Finally, just as there can be two correct answers to some mathematical problems, so there can be more than one solution to other problems. How then do you know which solution to choose? Again, the Four-way Test should help you decide—take the solution that brings the greatest benefit to you *and* to others.

THE MAGIC OF PROBLEM SOLVING

There is a magic to problem solving—the same kind of magic there is in playing baseball or any other sport. The more you practice, the better you become at it.

Some people never try to solve their own problems. Instead they go to counselors. A business may go to a management consultant. There is nothing wrong with that, for counselors and consultants are specialists who work on the solution of special kinds of problems. But why not try solving some of your own problems yourself? Then if you need help, go to those who have special experience and training.

Usually within each business there is a person to whom everyone goes with his or her problems, the same way children take their problems to their mother or father because this person seems to specialize in solving problems. And because he does this so often, he becomes good at it, again, like the baseball player who keeps practicing.

Problem solving can be fun. It can add spice to what would otherwise be boredom. It can lead to new ways of doing things, new inventions, new ways of making money, of finding shortcuts, of saving time and energy, and best of all, of securing new friendships and cementing old ones in ways nothing else could.

I strongly urge you to start solving your problems now. You have no idea how easy and fulfilling it is until you try and act.

WHAT ABOUT PROBLEMS YOU CAN'T SOLVE?

While I said earlier I believe there is a solution for every problem, I am well aware that many problems have not been solved and that you and I will not be able to solve all of our own problems. But we can solve most of them. And the more we become involved with problem solving, the greater will become our capacity for solving problems. They should be thought of as challenges rather than as problems.

Today, problems are being solved that our ancestors generations ago thought could never be solved. And today we have new problems that seem to defy a solution (i.e., how to handle nuclear waste).

Daryl Stingley is a man who knows how to live with a problem. Stingley, a star wide receiver with the New England Patriots, was paralyzed from the waist down as a result of a vicious hit in a football game. Though flat on his back, Stingley refuses to give up. Here's what he says about the agony of trying to lift even small weights: "Naturally, the pain means there's feeling there. I kind of developed a philosophy about pain: I like to feel pain because pain makes a man think, and thinking makes a man wise, and knowledge and wisdom are the keys to a peaceful life. All of a sudden I'm a glutton for pain."

Stingley knows he may never lick his problem, may never walk again or even have full use of his arms. But he keeps on trying, exercising five days a week: "It's like walking into a dark tunnel. You never know what's at the end. But you keep walking."

I keep in touch with Inez Compton, mother of my best friend, Glen, who was killed in a tragic accident some years ago.

Awhile back, Inez's mother was about to undergo a serious operation. On top of that,

Inez had recently lost her younger brother. I gave Inez a call to see how she was doing. Her answer is an inspiration to me anytime problems seem to weigh heavily. She said: "I'm feeling okay. Matter of fact, I'm feeling fine. When I get to feeling down or like my problems are too much, I get in my car and drive to the part of town where the people are less fortunate than I am. Then I drive home to my little mansion." (Inez's "mansion" is a small, four-room home.)

You may have personal and business problems you find impossible to solve, even with the help of counselors and consultants. But do not despair. Have faith that God will grant you the vision to solve these problems. He will give you the strength to live with them. I believe this with my whole heart.

UNIT

IV

PREPARING

FIFTEEN
Prepare and Your Chance Will Come

Don't wait for success. It is waiting for you! When opportunity knocks, you are the one who must open the door.

I firmly believe that people make their own success or failure. Far too often they sit around waiting for success to come to them, believing it is a game of chance. If they are lucky, they will be successful; if they are not, well then, they will fail.

Life is full of opportunities, some of which we generate ourselves and some of which are available to us through the grace of God. But whether or not we seize them is entirely up to us.

Life is also full of excuses: "I am too old," "I don't have time," "I don't know how," "I'm not able to," and the list goes on and on. If we are honest with ourselves, we know we are *not* too old, we *do* have time, we *can* learn how to do it if we want to, and in spite of physical problems, there *are* ways we can do most of whatever is before us. But we have to *want* to do something strongly enough to destroy these excuses and others like them.

It is ironic that as we mature and grow older we find it easy to come up with excuses to limit our involvement and action. The child, however, who lacks knowledge and know-how because of his young age, displays a great deal of self-confidence and assurance when he is struck by an idea that intrigues him. You can't hold him down. He is all energy, impatient to begin. Fear and doubt are beyond his imagination. It is a sad commentary on maturity that we allow the spirit of youth to dissipate and our energies to wane as we grow older.

If success and opportunity are going to be dependent on something other than luck, then we have to control the action. There are things we must do, responsibilities we must assume. Goal setting and planning must come early.

SETTING GOALS
We have said much about goals and their importance to motivation in earlier chapters of this book. Now we should take a moment

to highlight some of the things we know about them.

There are basically two types of goals: personal ones and professional ones. Personal goals concern what you set for yourself to do or to become. Professional goals are those you set for your profession or business. These goals are interdependent: You can't reach your personal goals without reaching your professional goals because the latter have to do with how you plan to make a living, which in turn affects the quality of your personal life. Sometimes personal and professional goals conflict; you are the one who will have to decide which goals have higher priority.

Goals, too, must be kept alive. A goal you set for yourself five years ago may not be realistic today because of changes in your life and in your wants. Five years ago you may have been single with no thoughts of marriage. Yet today you may be married with a couple of children, and your goals may have changed, or should be changed.

Your business may have grown at such a fast rate that it achieved in three years what you had originally thought it would accomplish in five. So what are the goals for your company now?

Yes, goals have to be kept alive; they need revising from time to time.

Dreaming is an excellent way to define goals. I have seen people suddenly throw away a job, move miles away, and become involved in something new just because they allowed themselves to dream a bit, and while doing so, they convinced themselves they could make their dreams come true.

But goals must be realistic. If you are four feet, six inches tall, you will never become a heavyweight champion regardless of how hard you study boxing. And you're not likely to become a jockey if you are six feet, four inches tall, no matter how much you love horses. You have to use good judgment in determining your goals; they must be within reason.

And they must be ethically and morally sound, for these are the only kinds that respond to positive thinking. Positive thinking does not aid a person breaking into a bank or trying to commit a fraud.

There is something else to remember about goals: It is never too late to establish them. Never. Herman Smith-Johannsen cross-country skis a mile a day when he can. That's his goal. And Mr. Smith-Johannsen is 105 years old! Catherine Clark, starting with a small bakery, built it into the multimillion-dollar Brownberry Ovens. Now, at seventy-three, she's ready to take on new challenges, new adventures.

PLANNING TO REACH YOUR GOALS

Goals are targets. Plans are blueprints for action to hit the targets and bring about the realization of your goals.

There are certain steps you should take in drawing up your plan of action:

1. Be specific.

2. Make long- and short-range plans.

3. Set sub-goals to shoot for.

4. Be prepared to adapt your plan to changing conditions.

5. Use reflection to refine and strengthen your plan.

The Need to Be Specific. At the end of the basketball court there is a steel hoop eighteen inches in diameter and ten feet above the floor. Unless the ball goes through the hoop, it doesn't count as a score.

Relative to the size of the ball and the court, that's a pretty small space, just eighteen inches in diameter and ten feet above the floor. And its location is very specific.

A goal plan needs to be specific, too. If your goal is to become a doctor, that doesn't say much, for there are scores of different kinds of doctors: Ph.D.'s, M.D.'s, D.C.'s, D.M.D.'s, D.M.L.'s, etc. So your goal is not just to earn any kind of doctor's degree. You want some more specific kind of degree. Let's assume it's an M.D. (Doctor of Medicine). That tells a great deal, and now you have the basis for setting up your plan. It must be a plan to become a medical doctor. Let's continue this illustration for our discussion of planning, although the principle can apply to any other field.

So you want to be an M.D. But you can be even more specific than that. Perhaps you wish to specialize in a particular area, pediatrics, for example. And perhaps your specialty in pediatrics is not general pediatrics but in children's bone diseases.

Now it becomes much easier to lay out your specific plans to reach your goal of becoming a pediatrician specializing in bone problems. Using positive thinking and focusing, you can now zero right in on your real goal and plan your way to it.

Long- and Short-Term Planning. When we think of long-range planning, we think of all the things we'll ever need to do. For instance, to become an M.D. you have to go to undergraduate school where you will take a premedical course, then on to medical school, then to internship. Next comes specializing in pediatrics, and finally specializing in bone diseases. None of these steps can be skipped. Timing is very important, and along with each of these steps you will want to include the length of time it will take to complete it, whether or not you may wish to take a year off to earn money, how old you will be when you finish, and similar factors.

Regardless of what your goal is, your plans should be as specific as in the foregoing illustration. Your business or professional goals and your personal goals should be identified and planned just as specifically. No step can be skipped.

MOTIVATIONAL MEMO
A wise man will make more opportunity than he finds. —Bacon

But there are also short-term plans you will have to make in order to reach your main goals. Short-term plans for the medical student might include a weekly schedule like this: five hours daily of classroom instruction, three hours a week of laboratory, a daily hour of exercise, four hours each night for study, and seven hours a night of sleep.

These, of course, are subject to change from time to time, but they do set forth how the medical student is going to plan his days in order to make progress toward his goal of being a specialized pediatrician.

Short-term plans can also be set up for a business by specifying such things as what new product is going to be put on the market and when; how many new employees are going to be on the payroll, when, and for what jobs; when the company plans to expand and in what way; and other similar considerations.

Time Targets. Short-term planning is essentially the setting up of sub- or intermediate goals along your route to reach your main goal. It becomes apparent, then, that it is necessary to have time targets for each of the steps of your short-term plan. These of course can be changed as circumstances dictate. However, these time targets should be respected and not changed unless it becomes urgent to do so. Changing time targets can have a disastrous effect if it becomes an exercise in delaying the necessary action to achieve your goals.

Subgoals provide a psychological lift when they are reached on time. Whatever you do, you need encouragement along the way, and the best encouragement is when you can take pride in something you have accomplished yourself. Reaching a subgoal is then an occasion to pat yourself on the back and feel good about your progress. It gives you encouragement and enthusiasm to go on to reach the next subgoal. Constantly postponing the subgoal is a sign of poor or unrealistic planning and offers little enthusiasm for honest perseverance. If your doctor tells you to lose forty pounds, for example, it's unrealistic to set a goal of taking all the extra weight off in a month. That's an almost impossible goal, and when you fail to reach it, you'll be totally demoralized. Better to take a sensible approach and set a goal of losing a pound or two a week.

Adapting Your Plan to Changing Conditions. Planning is a dynamic activity. It must be realistic, and being realistic requires that you constantly take into consideration any new factors that may relate to it. In the fast-paced world we live in, we can expect new factors to arise frequently.

John Mackovic, who was responsible for turning Wake Forest's football fortunes around, has this to say about the need to be flexible in planning and goal setting: "Get a plan and follow it. You may think you are destined to be an All-American college quarterback and wind up as a safety on defense, but you will still have something positive to show."

Mackovic stresses the importance of determination in sticking to your goals when he talks about Brian Piccolo, who was his teammate when he played at Wake Forest. "Brian led the nation in rushing and in points scored as a senior. Yet when the National Football League drafted 400 players that year, Brian was not among them. He wanted to play professional football. It was his dream. One day he heard from George Halas of the Chicago Bears, who sought him as a free agent. Brian was elated, and he went on to become a regular with the Bears. He died of cancer, a young man of twenty-six."

Major changes in the economy may require a time-target; a particular goal may need to be accelerated or retarded. A natural disaster or a death in the family may necessitate a change in goals or subgoals. There are many other factors that could also relate to goals and their timing: financial matters, moving the household to another state, serious illness, competitive products suddenly coming into the market, or a new federal regulation, just to mention a few.

But the very act of recognizing changing conditions can also be an easy or face-saving excuse not to face up to some hardship in reaching your goal. This must not be allowed to happen. The challenge of problems should be met head-on, there should be constant refocusing on your goals, and they should be faced with enthusiasm, positively. Nevertheless, it is unrealistic not to consider the effects of changing conditions upon goals and your plan for reaching them.

Reflection. Just as a quiet time for daily meditation and prayer is good for a person's spiritual life, so also is a daily period of reflection good for a person to think about his goals. This helps to keep goals uppermost in the mind and provides valuable time to focus on their accomplishment.

Such periods of reflection can be very productive in generating new ideas, in revising or updating goals. It is a period of self-motivation. And it is especially valuable to keep the lines of action tight if there has been some setback in your plans. Reflection is the cure for discouragement at such times, for if you are able through reflection to *adjust* to a situation, you will find that the situation, more often than not, can be used to your advantage; you will be far less speculative in your planning and more sure of productive action.

In the final analysis, nothing good is built without a plan. And no plan is better than the constant thought that goes into it. Even the successful architect updates his plans during the building process to accept new and better materials when they are brought onto the market.

SIXTEEN
Use Your Time More Wisely

Time is your most precious commodity. It's worth everything to you, and it must be used wisely. None of us knows how much time he has left, and time that is wasted in nonproductive activities is time that can never be regained.

There is a saying that "yesterday is a cancelled check, tomorrow is a promissory note. Only today is cash in hand."

Whatever your goals are, they must be accomplished in the remaining time you have, so the way you occupy your time should be of paramount interest to you. With forethought and action, you can make your time pay high dividends, whether it is time spent in work or time spent in leisure.

You can lose a thousand dollars and get it back, but lost time is gone forever.

LEISURE TIME

It is easy to think of leisure time as wasted time. It may be, but doesn't have to be.

The body and the mind have need of relaxation. Often, when we leave for vacation, we are tired and edgy. Work has gotten us down, and we long to get away from the phone and the people. We want a complete change from the working day. By the time we return to work, our batteries are recharged, so to speak; we have renewed spirits, and once again we know how to practice patience and tolerance.

This has not been wasted time but rather time for recreation and re-creation—time to become reacquainted with ourselves and with nature.

While it may not have been productive in terms of your business, it has been productive in terms of restoring your body and mind. It would be good advice to spend some time each day in leisurely pursuits to balance the extremes of the daily workload.

A TIME TO WORK

Since so much of our time is spent working, either directly or indirectly, and since time is so valuable to us in achieving our goals, we should consider what robs us of productive time and what contributes to improving time's productivity.

Time Wasters. People who are expert in the management of time usually suggest that interested persons record in a notebook exactly what they did each fifteen minutes of the day for several days or for a couple of weeks. Then they analyze their notes, and most are surprised to find that they have been victimized by time wasters such as the following:

Being late for appointments. I am constantly amazed at how frequently people are late for appointments. Usually it is the same people. Others have to sit around and wait until they arrive, and it is not unusual for a cumulative hour or more of productive time to be lost by all involved in the appointment. And such people seldom have the thoughtfulness to apologize, knowing full well that next time they will be late as usual. Be honest. Does this description fit you? If so, think about how *you* feel when you are kept waiting. You don't like it, right? Others don't like it any better than you do. And the solution to tardiness is so simple: Just think of the time you need to leave—and leave fifteen minutes earlier.

Chit-chat and coffee breaks. If you find you are wasting a lot of time gabbing with fellow employees, hanging around the water cooler, getting coffee, and waiting for the mail rather than actually working, you're obviously not making good use of your time. And you are probably wasting someone else's time as well. You should think hard about your job: Are you bored? Do you need to change employment to something more exciting to you? Be frank; it is you who will lose out if you waste so much time.

Distractions and interruptions. Some interruptions are unavoidable; if the boss calls you into his office, you'd better go. But often interruptions are caused by coworkers dropping in to chat, personal telephone calls, reviewing the news of the day, exchanging rumors. Your coworkers will respect you, however, if you are firm and request that they not disturb you.

Indecision. What a lot of time is wasted through indecision—the inability to act promptly, especially when you are faced with two or more alternatives of seemingly equal importance. But action is better than inaction, and you will get ahead much faster by making a decision one way or another than by wasting more time plowing the same ground.

Worry. Worry is one of the greatest time wasters. What we have already said in chapter 9 about worrying may well be applied here.

Putting things off. Putting things off is closely allied to worry. It is often the result of worry. It is also closely allied to indecision. But postponing does not get rid of the problem; it only delays it until it may well balloon into other problems. Immediate action, even though it may result in extra work, is much better than pushing action off until a later day.

Meetings and committees. I know of few activities that waste more time than meetings and committees. The natural tendency is for them to drag on and on until people become bored, and no bright ideas emerge. But they can be shortened and made to be responsive and valuable. First, there should be a promise to start on time and to *end* on time, and this promise should be respected. There should be an agenda with responsibilities for each item assigned to members of the meeting. They should not only have time to prepare but should also come prepared. The person moderating the meeting or chairing the committee should be forceful in following the agenda and keeping the agenda moving. And the number attending or being on the committee should be as small as possible. Consider, too, when meetings should be held. I know a particular monthly meeting that failed until it was changed to the breakfast hour, at which time it was completed in plenty of time for the day's business to start.

The long lunch hour. Beware the long lunch hour if you are trying to save time. True, time can be saved by using the lunch hour for conferences and meetings, but there is a tendency to set up lunch dates in town at the cost of hours of lost time. It runs like this: a half hour at least to get from the office to a restaurant, fifteen minutes to wait for your guest, at least two hours over lunch, and another half hour to return to the office. Three hours and fifteen minutes—of which only one hour has probably been productive!

Auditing Your Time. I agree with management engineers that using a notebook to record how you spend your time is one of the best ways to audit this activity. Even though you feel you are an efficient person, you will find new ways to improve this efficiency if you will make a periodic audit of how you spend your time.

For example, a friend of mine who had just taken over the presidency of an active division of a large company was bothered by the great length of time it required for letters sent to his division to be answered. People would phone him saying that such and such a person had not answered letters sent in two weeks previously. The division head decided to study the problem, starting with his own desk. His study resulted in the following plan, which he insisted everyone in his division follow:

1. There should be only two mail boxes on a person's desk: an in-box and an out-box. The "hold" box should be dispensed with immedi-

ately, for this was where the unanswered letters were piling up.

MOTIVATIONAL MEMO
You'll find that restructuring your time and using it efficiently is itself a motivational aid. It will enable you immediately to get more done—i.e., to be more successful.

2. All mail that comes in must be answered within twenty-four hours.

3. Even if there was insufficient information at hand to answer the incoming mail, it was at least acknowledged within twenty-four hours, and the original writer was assured when he could expect an answer.

4. Also, in cases where there was insufficient information for a reply, the writer's letter and other pertinent information traveled together to the person who could supply the information. When it was returned, the entire file was there in one location, making it easier to draft a reply.

5. When a letter could not be answered for lack of ready information, the person responsible for the reply noted on his calendar the date he had promised the writer a reply, or his secretary would flag it in her suspense file.

This system bore fruit immediately. Customers were delighted with the streamlined communications system, and they told the president they preferred to do business with his organization because they were kept informed promptly. And I am told that this system got much *new* business for this division from its competitors because people always felt informed. But don't overlook the big point here: hours and hours of time were saved, for no one had to spend time, days after a letter was received, to reorient himself to the problem of the inquiry or to spend time answering letters from irate customers who had received no reply.

Time Savers. My own business experience has taught me many useful ways to save time. At the risk of some repetition, I would like to share them with you. I strongly urge you to be watchful of ways you can increase your time. Test them out, and if they work, use them. But if they don't, chuck them and look for other ways.

—Be on time, and require others to be on time.

—Write short memos, right to the point. If you are asking for a reply, the answer should be written on the memo you sent out.

—If meetings with other people are required, have them at an hour that does not interfere with business hours, if possible. Start on time and end on time. Always come to the meeting with a specific agenda.

—Delegate authority and responsibility. Allow others to be managers. And do expect some mistakes, for that is the way promising people learn.

—Use a calendar to keep you up-to-date. Note all commitments you make; then forget about them until the calendar brings them up. If you need a couple of days to prepare for a commitment, note those days on the calendar as well. Then respect the integrity of your calendar and others will also.

—The telephone is a valuable machine. Use it wisely. Call when you can to save time rather than dictating a letter or memo. Be pleasant but keep chit-chat to a minimum.

Punctuality. Punctuality is a promise that you will be at a certain place at a certain time. Remember that; it is a promise you made. Therefore, if you wish your word to be honored, you must honor your word.

If you are delayed through no fault of your own, it takes such a small amount of energy to notify those who are inconvenienced if you must be late, and to do so is an acknowledgment that you want your word to be honored and depended on.

Punctuality puts you in command; it also shows you recognize that time is indeed your most precious commodity and that you know how to make the best use of it.

SEVENTEEN
Know the Secret of Success

Success is a philosophy of life, and I wish to share my philosophy with you. It begins with love.

Material things and success are not the same. I know far too many people who have accumulated wealth and status, but who live in constant fear of losing both. And I know others whose material possessions are small, who have little fame, but who possess happiness beyond the dreams of many. I call the former failures, but I see success in the latter.

Richard Chavez is president of Richard Chavez Associates, one of the country's leading vocational institutions for the handicapped and disadvantaged. Richard, a polio victim who is himself disabled, had a terrific definition of success:

Success is defined in different ways. Some see it in money, power, fame. But it's also the concept of "reaching down," of being able to help your fellowman. Material things you can buy and sell, but things like hope and courage and faith and knowledge are gifts you give your fellowman to pull him up. Whatever you give out to others will come back. It may take a while, but it will come back.

HAPPINESS AND LOVE

Are happiness and love the same? They should be, but then it's a different kind of happiness from what we commonly think. I do believe that my kind of happiness and love are the same. There is a certain satisfaction, mental and spiritual, that one gets from love. Love may involve heartbreaks and struggles; yet there is something holy about it, something that removes it from the common things of life. I believe that true happiness has this same quality that love has—a holy aspect that transcends struggles and heartbreaks.

What do love and happiness have in common that give them this feeling of holiness? People! The answer is people!

We do not live in a personal vacuum. We live in a society where we have to mingle with others in order to exist. Any degree of love we feel, or any degree of happiness, must involve our attitudes and actions toward others.

Success must also involve others. Certainly self-esteem is positive; we need self-esteem to exist, but that is only half the picture. The other half is people, people with whom we come in contact daily, people who are affected by our actions, people who are recipients of our love. It is difficult, if not impossible, to achieve success without the goodwill of others. I believe there is no such thing as a self-made man. You will never become successful without the help of others. And others must love you to help you to the top.

SUCCESS AND POSITIVE GOALS

If we have good goals and work toward achieving them, we shall be successful. This does not mean we shall achieve every goal we set out to meet; but most of them will be fulfilled.

As we have said before, goals must be realistic and reflect good judgment. They involve hard work. It requires of us that we analyze ourselves and determine our weaknesses, which must be overcome through self-evaluation and effort. Then we must act positively by focusing on the fulfillment of our goals.

But unless our goals involve others—people with whom we live and work and intermingle in our daily lives—they can be selfish and unrewarding. The fulfillment of our goals must be good for others; if they bring harm to others, then our goals are selfish, and we can expect no blessing from God.

But if our goals are positive and considerate of others, even though there may be struggles and problems along the way, I believe we are headed toward success.

We make things happen—things just don't happen by themselves. We have a responsibility in fulfilling our goals to be certain that good is accomplished and that whatever is achieved, be it material wealth, wisdom, or whatever, is used for the advantage of others as well as for our own.

It has been well said that "money will buy things that are for sale, and happiness is not one of them. The great rewards in life are *love* and achievement. All else is secondary." This I believe. This is success.

THE REBOUND FROM LOVE

Success then is really love in its purest sense. When you have learned to love—really love—everything and everybody, you have found happiness and the secret of success.

We've said a lot about action in this book,

and we'll say a lot more about it because action is what motivation is. We want to become enthusiastic about doing something. I point this out because we must realize that love is an empty word if there is no action.

Loving life is a two-way street all the way. We don't receive good service if we don't serve with love. We don't receive care and compassion if we don't extend them to others. We don't receive respect and love from spouse and children if we don't give them respect and love. Call it the "yo-yo effect" or think of it as a bouncing rubber ball; it comes back to us only after we send it forth.

There is, however, a strange and wonderful thing about the plenty which love returns to the sender; it comes back in far greater strength and intensity than that in which it was sent forth. Its strength is multiplied many times, bringing with it an abundant harvest.

MOTIVATIONAL MEMO
Getters generally don't get happiness; givers get it. —Charles H. Burr

Why then should we be satisfied with keeping love locked up within ourselves where it will lie dormant and die from non-use? The only way to be successful and happy, whether in personal, business, or professional life, is to send forth love; success and happiness will come on the rebound.

That is the secret to success. Success is judged by your degree of happiness. And happiness is determined by how much you give away.

EIGHTEEN
Develop an Ability to Communicate

There are many ways we communicate or endeavor to transfer our thoughts and wishes to others. And there are many ways that others respond to our communications. *The person who is motivated to get ahead must understand the principles of good communication.*

HOW DOES COMMUNICATION WORK?
Any method we use to transfer a message, voluntarily or involuntarily, from ourselves to others is a method of communication. We may use verbal communication, such as a written letter or message, or we may use oral communication, as with speech. We can tap out codes on ham radio sets, and we can use hand signals. Our facial expressions may transmit messages of pain or bereavement or happiness or doubt or fear. We may tremble

to show fright, and convey a message of pain if we walk with crutches. Running toward a guest denotes great pleasure in seeing that person, the master patting a dog shows love as does the wedding ceremony and a couple walking hand- in-hand in the moonlight. A mother feeling the brow of an ill child indicates love and concern.

There simply is no end to the number of ways messages and feelings are communicated from one person to another.

Neither is there an end to the many ways a person responds to a communication.

A parent may tell a child to come into the house, and if the child likes the tone of the parent's voice, he will come in immediately with great expectation of cookies or some other surprise. If the parent's voice is sharp or indignant, the child may interpret the very same words of the parent to mean he has done something wrong and will be punished. A listless "Come into the house" will convey the thought that it is not really necessary to come in, and a stern voice can indicate that harm is about to befall a child who remains outside.

THE PROBLEMS OF COMMUNICATING
The problems of communicating are many. We may wish to convey a certain message,

only to be betrayed by our own contradictory facial expression. Or our message may be misinterpreted by the receiver because of his own shyness, his stubbornness, his mental and physical condition at the moment, or by many other factors. Perhaps, too, our message was not specific; it may have failed to make its point. Or it may have contradicted a previous instruction without any explanation. In short, failure to get the right message across to the receiver is due to one or both of the following:

1. Failure of the communicator to send the message properly.

2. Failure of the receiver to interpret the message properly.

There are those who believe with great justification that all problems of the family and the world are caused by bad communication. This may seem like an exaggeration at first, but if you think for a moment, you will realize that no problem is solved until *after* both sides start communicating with each other.

The importance of effective communication is well illustrated by a football team. Imagine the resulting disaster if the team had no play signals! No one would know what the other was doing. The team would have no common direction. There would be chaos.

HOW TO COMMUNICATE

There are certain time-tested ways to communicate that everyone should be aware of if he or she wishes to be interpreted correctly:

1. *Tell the truth.* Do not attempt to deceive in any way. Too often a person will set a trap for himself by misrepresenting a situation or product, hoping that the receiver will be misled as to all the facts.

2. *Get to the point quickly and directly.* Skirting the issue and dilly-dallying only confuse the issue and encourage the receiver to believe there is some hidden meaning in the communication that is not good for him. So plan ahead what you wish to say and keep it simple.

3. *Respect the receiver's point of view.* Honest differences are important in life, and we'll have to live with some of them. Everybody has them. They sharpen debate and help to locate the common ground on which to start building understanding. A communication that fails to recognize the receiver's point of view is not only confusing the issue; it is also treating the receiver rudely.

4. *Criticism will get you nowhere.* It serves only to heighten the resistance of the receiver. The positive substitute for criticism is counseling, honestly helping the receiver to understand the problem being discussed.

5. *Don't take people for granted.* No two

people are alike; no two have identical back-grounds or the same inward feelings. Try to understand human nature and human behavior. Treat each person as a special case.

6. *Listen and see.* The response of the receiver can tell a great deal about his thoughts and feelings. Listen to his words, but, more than that, listen to the tone of his voice, to the forcefulness of his manner, to the directness of his reply. These may convey much more of his feeling than the actual words uttered.

7. *Ask questions to be certain the receiver understands you.*

THE ROLE OF THE RECEIVER

The receiver, the person being communicated with, should also make a real effort to understand the message being sent to him. The following should help:

1. *Listen.* Nothing is more important than listening. Listen to the entire message before accepting or rejecting it. Far too often we jump to conclusions, only to find out that we formed our opinion on only a segment of the information being sent to us.

2. *Give the communicator your full attention.* Participating in the distractions fragments the communicator's message and leads to confusion, immature judgments, and misunderstandings.

3. *Ask questions.* If there is any doubt what-

soever about the message or its intent and purpose, question the communicator before giving a final answer or making judgment. State your interpretation of the message and ask if your interpretation is correct.

LEADERSHIP

No one can be a successful leader who does not endeavor to communicate effectively. The ability to communicate is a must for good leadership. This is not always an easy matter, but persistent effort and practice will produce amazingly fast results. Confusion and problems are the reward of him who does not take communications seriously—confusion and problems that breed more of their kind and rob one of valuable time spent in trying to straighten out misunderstandings.

MOTIVATIONAL MEMO
Good communicators often become great leaders. You, too, can become a leader through precise, thoughtful communication. Remember: A boss says, "Get going!" A leader says, "Let's go!"

There are other qualities of good leaders, which, while not necessarily specific for good communications, will contribute greatly to people who are working to improve their communication:

1. *Be generous in rewarding others.* There are two ways to motivate people to do things—reward and punishment. Punishment is degrading and provides a ready backlash for the leader. The atmosphere becomes negatively charged, and until this negative atmosphere is removed, nothing productive is accomplished, nor will the leader have the support and loyalty he needs, nor can communication take place. Psychologists who have studied motivation know that reward has much greater motivating power than punishment. It establishes a common bond with the leader, a positive bond that encourages effective cooperation. Good communications, also, should include rewards. A willingness to consider an opposing point of view is a reward for the receiver. So are compliments for his trying to understand a point of view he does not accept. The leader will look for ways to reward the receiver, such as praise and compliments that are honest and deserved.

2. *Delegation.* No one can aspire to leadership who does not delegate authority. This is the true test of leadership and also the prime compliment to those to whom authority is delegated. Delegation is a reward that says, "I trust you!" It is a recognition of confidence and faith. How does delegation relate to effective communication? The answer is also a question: How can one assume authority if he cannot be

the chief communicator on that over which he has authority? The good leader will set forth the policies he wants implemented, but he will not be the one who provides the detailed communication. He'll leave that to others.

3. *Forget yourself.* The most important concern of a leader is the other fellow, the person he leads. And his ability to know the other fellow will be his ability to communicate with him effectively when he forgets himself and makes the other the important one.

4. *Study human behavior.* This is the key to interacting with other people—knowing what makes them act as they do and knowing what you can do about it. There is a vast fund of research on behavioral science, and the successful leader and communicator will learn all he can to increase his effectiveness through his knowledge of human nature.

NINETEEN
Be Independent But Be Yourself

While motivated people know they need the support of others to succeed, they take responsibility for their own lives; they are not afraid to think and act for themselves. When a person is unable to stand alone, he uses a crutch or a cane. We drive along the highway and notice poles supported by guy lines, trees that require posts to hold up their branches, and piles of rocks that prevent a hillside from falling into the sea.

There is nothing wrong with this, but remember what happens at some future time when the supports are withdrawn. Without cane or crutch, the physically impaired person is frozen—unable to walk by himself. When the guy lines rust or are suddenly cut off, the poles fall under their own weight; branches break when their supports are removed; and if the rocks are removed, the sea will claim the hillside.

MATURING

When we start out in life, we are almost totally supported by other people. Without such support, we would probably perish. Later, throughout school and college, we have teachers to guide us and give us security. If we are learning to swim, the instructor is there to teach us and come to our aid in emergencies.

But eventually these supports are going to be withdrawn, for time marches on, and if we are unable to stand on our own, we'll be as helpless as we were the day we were born. Therefore, we have a responsibility to ourselves to work toward independence so we can chuck our supports and go it alone. This is the process of maturing.

Responsibility. We are responsible for our own success in life. To be successful, we must mature and act for ourselves, not having always to rely on others to make decisions for us.

One does not become a responsible person overnight; in fact, it is a continuous growth process. But along the way we shed more and more of our supports until we finally stand on our own two feet, make our own decisions, and learn from the consequences.

Consistency. Part of maturation is the self-discipline to work consistently toward our goals. Here's what motivational author Arthur Mortell has to say about consistency:

> Few people can be consistent. Without being consistent, an individual will have only temporary financial success, never really be in good physical condition, be only partially involved with people, and never fulfill his spiritual potential.
>
> Where do we begin? First, take one area of life which is important and which can be measured. Make a decision that this area of your life is a symbol of consistency and say, "I can do this each day. I can prove that I can be consistent. If I can be consistent in one segment of my life, then I can confront other challenges with the same self-discipline."

Initiative. It is unrealistic to sit around waiting for breaks to come our way, for breaks are not part of the scenario. We must step out and help ourselves, feeling confident, courageous, and determined that we'll reach our goal of independence. We can do this by consistently motivating ourselves through positive thinking, self-discipline, and focusing on the independence we seek.

A woman who knows the value of independent, courageous action is Rose Cook

Small. Rose, who was born in 1912, grew up in a poor neighborhood in Camden, New Jersey. One of six children of poor immigrant parents, Rose peddled vegetables to help the family out. She had to leave school at an early age.

At sixteen, Rose married Harry Cook, who operated a local market. Working in the market with her husband, she began to build a dream of owning a large meat-packing business. Working long hours in the market until her hands were raw and red, and raising two children at the same time, Rose kept the dream alive.

Their business grew, and two years later they opened another market, this time with a packing house. But in 1937 a fire destroyed that market. So broke that she couldn't afford eight cents for trolley fare, Rose walked fourteen miles to the store to clean up and see what could be salvaged.

Finding the bank reluctant to lend the Cooks money to start over, Rose put up her wedding and engagement rings as collateral. Bluebird, Inc. was born in 1940 with the money Rose had obtained from her rings. The bluebird they chose as their symbol means love, grace, and happiness.

When Harry Cook died in 1950, Rose took over, filling the roles of mother, father, breadwinner, and advisor. She also carried on the business, directing its growth and expansion. Over the years Rose learned the business, from buying to slaughtering and cutting meats. At the same time, she put one of her sons through medical school. The other joined her in the business.

After years of bone-tiring work, this woman of independent spirit built Bluebird into a giant meat packer that produces 11 million pounds of meat weekly, with annual sales of over half a billion dollars.

MAKING THE RIGHT DECISIONS

Much of the process of maturing is concerned with making the right decisions. These affect progress toward our goals, and they also affect how well we work with other people. We begin with small decisions, using trial and error, much as aspiring athletes do when they practice. But these small decisions are important, for they condition us to bring judgment into our decisions. If we learn nothing from the trial-and-error method, we'll never improve, never be able to make bigger decisions, which is one of our goals. But trial and error must be analyzed: Why were we successful? Or, why did we fail? Now we begin to accumulate some knowledge about making decisions, some wisdom. We use the knowledge acquired as background for other decisions—bigger ones—and we analyze these bigger decisions and tuck some more wisdom back in our mind to rely on for even larger decisions. We begin to notice now that much of the acquired knowledge for making the right decisions comes into use almost automatically when we need it, our decisions become easier to arrive at, and as we gain wisdom, we notice that the percentage of our right decisions increases.

MOTIVATIONAL MEMO
Independence is a constant adjustment to today, letting go of old things, but building on the strengths of yesterday to meet the challenges of tomorrow.

The importance of recognizing the outcome of our decisions is not to be underestimated, for this is the way we develop our ability to gain independence and to come closer to a goal of good decision making.

Does your decision have a positive effect on others? Does it help you? If it does not meet those two criteria, it is the wrong decision, and you should know where you went wrong. Once you know this, you can avoid making the error in the future. But if you did make the right decision according to these criteria, remember how you did it. The reasoning here is also important and should be tucked away in your memory for future use. *Making the right decision contributes to your wisdom only if you are aware of why you made a good decision and use this information for future guidance.*

No one suddenly becomes good at decision making. It requires practice—constant practice, just as learning to skate requires practice. Practice is the basis of improvement. How can you avoid falling down again? How do you do the figure eight? The spin? In skating, falling down is necessary to know how not to fall down. And in decision making, falling is sometimes necessary to help you make the right decision.

THE STATE OF INDEPENDENCE
What is the state of independence to which you aspire?

We talk a lot about independence, but the more independent we become, the more we realize we become more and more involved with other people and with the problems of the company with which we work. Independence, then, is not isolation. Independence is developing your own self toward being able to act and act right.

Being independent also means not relying on the opinion of others for your feelings of your own self-worth. Constantly seeking the approval of others before you act is not independence. You must develop your own idea of self-worth. Neither should you rely on others to make up your mind for you. Being tolerant of others, of learning their points of view and taking wise advice is far different from adopting the results of opinion polls, of jumping onto fads, and of accepting the unquestioned opinions of one's peers.

But, again, this does not mean you avoid the opinions and advice of others; indeed not. Or that you avoid reading books that contain helpful information and suggestions, or that you avoid conferences where useful information is dispensed. Independence means that you accumulate wisdom and knowledge from all these sources, but when action is required, *you* initiate the action, *you* make the decisions, *you* accept the consequences. Independence is responsibility; you, not somebody else, is the person who gets the praise or the blame for what you decide to do.

Finally, independence requires an ability to accept change and to accommodate change. This is a changing world; things happen fast. What was good for yesterday is not always good for today. You cannot lean on old times anymore than you can lean on others to make your decisions for you. I believe no one should invest time or money in some field or line of endeavor that is out of harmony with the times. Think ahead—use good judgment.

TWENTY
You Can Succeed in Business

Harvey Firestone, one of the great industrialists of our country, had this to say:

> Capital isn't so important in business. Experience isn't so important. You can get both these things. What is important is ideas. If you have ideas, you have the main asset you need, and there isn't any limit to what you can do with your business and your life. They are any man's greatest asset—ideas.

I find it difficult to refute that statement. If capital is needed to support a business, a lending institution will provide that if you can demonstrate that your company is alert, energetic, creative, and responsible. If you lack experience, there are management consulting organizations that can supply what you lack in experience, whether it be production, marketing, financing know-how, or whatever you need. But if you need ideas for a business, ideas for a product, ideas for something to sell, you have to provide them yourself if you expect to be successful.

One such idea came to George Ballas as he drove his car through a car wash. As he watched the strings of the brushes envelop and surround his car, his mind relaxed and turned to thoughts of home, of finishing the tedious chore of trimming and edging his lawn, down on his hands and knees.

Then, *bingo*. An idea. *The* idea. "I'd been trying to think of some way to trim the grass around trees and patio stones on my lawn, and suddenly it came to me. I noticed how the strings in the car wash straighten out when revolving at high speed, yet . . . were flexible enough to reach into every nook and cranny." Thus was born the Weedeater!

Back home, Ballas punched holes in a popcorn can and threaded the holes with cord. Then he took the blade off his edger and bolted the can in place. Ballas remembers that his invention tore up the turf and made a loud noise, "but it did the job I wanted."

At first Ballas intended to use his trimmer himself, because he couldn't afford yard help and "anyway, no one would take the job. My house is near a bayou, and who wants to get down on his hands and knees and trim around rocks when a copperhead snake might be hiding there?"

When he decided to go commercial, the going was rough. He was turned down by the first twenty distributors he approached. They would say, "Cut grass with a nylon string? You must be crazy!"

So in 1971 Ballas invested his money in the first thirty-pound Weedeater. Using a home-made commercial filmed by his son, he went out and bought twelve thousand dollars' worth of local TV air time. He was swamped with calls: "I think there must have been a convention in town at the time because calls started coming in from all over."

From that improbable beginning, Weed-eater, Inc., has grown into a multimillion-dollar international corporation in just a few short years. And it all started with a bright idea in a car wash.

WHAT KIND OF BUSINESS?

Since earning a living requires the majority of one's time, serious thought should be given to the type of work one would like to be involved in as an employee or an entrepreneur. All too often this is given far too little thought. When you realize that earning a living will consume a large part of your life, it becomes an important matter.

I cannot overemphasize the importance of doing something you believe in and enjoy. It is impossible to be successful if you are going to be bored and unhappy. Not only will your work suffer, but your disposition will also; and people with whom you work will be affected by your restlessness.

There is little motivation if you choose a business that makes you unhappy. And you will earn no rewards. I have seen far too many people try to become sales representatives, for example, thinking that they can adjust to any situation. But when they discovered that the job required them to travel away from home over a hundred nights a year, there was no longer any enthusiasm for their work. In such instances, the sooner one quits and finds a business he or she likes, the better. A boring job breeds no ideas; *creativity* is an unknown word. And negative thinking becomes a strong temptation.

I am more and more convinced that a job that offers no motivation can reduce one to disappointment and frustration. If you are unhappy working in such a situation, recognize that now, get out, and find something you know you can be happy doing.

Look for challenge, for problems to be solved, for an arena in which to use your ideas and solve problems. Go where there is action—action that will not become a problem to you, your family, or your friends.

One woman who found something she could enjoy is Jeanenne Stimson, who parlayed her patchworking hobby into a thriving business. Just a few years ago, with her children growing up and with time on her hands, Jeanenne turned to the versatile craft of quilting, designing and making purses, potholders, glass cases, and the like. A short while later, Jeanenne started selling her work through gift shops and patchwork parties. The next step was craft fairs throughout the Midwest, where Jeanenne became known as the "Patchwork Lady." That name was to become the label for her products.

Patchwork Lady items are now sold in such department stores as Marshall Field and Company in Chicago. In the process, Jeanenne has created a twentieth-century cottage industry. Because she wants all Patchwork Lady products to be hand sewn, she employs dozens of women who sew the products in their homes. Meanwhile, Jeanenne takes care of the designing.

THE TRUE ASSETS OF A BUSINESS

When I mention true assets, I am talking about the intangible and nonfinancial assets a company has to have in order to become successful. Unfortunately, this kind of asset never appears on the financial reports of a company; yet its importance can eclipse the importance of financial assets.

I am talking about enthusiasm, for instance. There are businesses whose very walls shake with enthusiasm for its products or services it sells, and this enthusiasm comes from the people who work there. These businesses challenge their employees with opportunity and reward. In return, the employees have a chance to expand their own interests and to get ahead.

MOTIVATIONAL MEMO
No matter what you produce or sell, before you can become successful, you must first recognize that you are in the people business.

A most important asset is people—the better the people, the better the company. This is best exemplified by their determination to set goals and get ahead, by their ability to get along with others, by their willingness to cooperate, by their positive attitudes, and by their constant integrity and their initiative to get things done without constant supervision.

Ben Marcus, head of Milwaukee's Marcus Corporation, started with a single small-town movie theater, and now owns eighty-three—in addition to hotels, motels, and restaurants.

Together, these various enterprises produce some $80 million in revenue annually. Marcus says that in business

> the main thing is your people, the people who are operating your business. And that doesn't apply just to executives; I mean all the way down the line.
>
> You've got to like people to give the right kind of service, to do the right kind of job. To us, the usher in the theater, the fellow who cleans the lobbies, the girl who makes up the rooms are as important to us as our general managers. If any of these fail to do his job, it makes us look awfully bad.
>
> The main thing you have to learn is to delegate. You can't be a one-man show. You have to develop people—the kind of people who like the business.

Every product or service a business has to offer for sale had to be thought of at some time in the past. Typewriters, for instance, didn't suddenly materialize out of thin air and appear in some company's inventory. Someone had to think up the idea of a typewriter; others had ideas to perfect it. And in the future still others will come up with new ideas for further changes. Dry cleaning is a service; yet the dry cleaning processes didn't just happen by themselves. Someone had the ideas, and they were perfected and will be further perfected by people with imagination. Each of these—one a product and the other a service—was someone's brainstorm. And from these brainstorms came businesses to provide the product and the service for customers. And with them also came opportunities for employment and profit.

It is possible to teach a person to do almost anything. But you can't teach a person to think. This he must do for himself. And an employee who can think, not only for himself but for his company, is one of the most valuable assets a company can have.

THE TRUE LIABILITIES OF A COMPANY

A simplified way to think of a company's true liabilities is to think of the opposite of its true assets. Lack of enthusiasm, employees who have no imagination and no new ideas, employees with no determination and no integrity are examples of liabilities. Jealousy, backbiting, office politics, and dishonest maneuvering to get ahead are other examples.

Beware of businesses that cannot control their true liabilities; sooner or later they will end in failure (bankruptcy). They do not represent opportunities for the motivated person who wishes to get ahead.

YOU MAKE YOUR OWN OPPORTUNITIES

People make their own opportunities. How? By making themselves wanted by others.

A business wants a person who believes in the company, one who believes in its product or service, one who believes in the people with whom he will work.

It looks for a person who will work (and I mean truly work) whatever hours are necessary to get the job done, not a person whose interest is only putting in the required amount of time. This requires learning everything possible about the job. It also requires learning and growing professionally. This may involve additional study, the reading of professional journals, attending seminars and workshops. It certainly means keeping on top of the state of the art of one's profession.

It also requires a certain amount of independence—an ability to get things done without constant supervision and advice. Such a person must have self-confidence and dedication.

And very high on the list of necessary qualifications is to be a dependable, hard-working person with an action-oriented mind.

There are far too many instances today of people who have no interest in their jobs other than putting in the required number of hours each week and collecting their check. This type of person is a company liability and a cause of employee friction and trouble. Unless a company can make an honest profit, it cannot exist, and each worker should believe that or he will never have any respect for productivity.

So it behooves each employee to turn in honest and faithful work. Whenever the financial liabilities of a company exceed its financial assets, it is doomed to bankruptcy and likely demise. But the intangible liabilities mentioned above do not have to exceed the intangible assets before a company is in trouble. That is why good management is constantly looking for ways to strengthen its intangible assets, and management will want you and seek you out if you possess the qualifications it is searching for. And if you do, *you make your own opportunities.*

In short, you can succeed in business if you want to, if you are motivated and goal-oriented, and if you are willing to go into action and work to achieve your goals.

BEING THE PERSON YOU WOULD WANT TO HIRE

Many enterprising people will want to start their own businesses. Literally thousands of small businesses are started in this country each year, all by people who want to be successful and make a profit.

Suppose you are one of those people. What

kind of person would you be looking for? Where would you put your money? A person whose main interest is in putting in the nine-to-five hours? One with questionable integrity? One who has no enthusiasm for the job? One who requires constant supervision? A negative thinker who has no goals? One who cannot be challenged by problems? One with no self-confidence and no faith in himself? One who scorns productivity?

Of course you would have nothing to do with such applicants, for they have none of the qualities you require. You would spend all the time necessary to locate people who want to get ahead, those who would question whether there might be a better way of doing something, those who give you assurance of complete honesty and loyalty, and those who would be self-starters.

The person who interviews you is looking for the identical qualities you would be searching for if you were starting a business of your own. Think hard about yourself. Do you possess what is required for someone to want you? Would you hire yourself if you were applying for a position in your company? If not, it is not too late to review your plan, recast your goals, and reset your priorities.

V

USING
FAITH
AS A
POWER
SOURCE

TWENTY-ONE
Change Your Life with a Good Attitude

William James, the psychologist and philosopher, termed a "revolution" the discovery that human beings can change their lives by changing their attitudes.

ATTITUDE AND PERSONAL LIFE

I am convinced that nothing can stop the person with the right attitude toward achieving his personal goals in life. The right attitude directs one to use his abilities to gain the maximum from them.

Nowhere is this principle better illustrated than in the story of General Daniel "Chappy" James. The youngest of seventeen children, James was born in a poor black section of Pensacola in 1920.

Since Pensacola is the home of U.S. Naval Air, James grew up watching the sky full of naval training planes every day. At age twelve, he did odd jobs around an airport to earn plane rides and flying lessons. His dream was to fly for the navy, but at that time no blacks were allowed to become pilots in the armed services.

After high school James went to Tuskegee Institute, where he played football and earned a B.S. in physical education. In 1942 James completed pilot training at the Institute under the government-sponsored Civilian Pilot Training Program—a special program for black pilots. He served, until early 1943, as a civilian instructor in the Army Air Corps Aviation Cadet Program at Tuskegee, the first program to train black aviators for the Air Corps.

James then earned his commission as a second lieutenant in the Air Corps. For the next six years, he served with various fighter squadrons in the United States. At the time, black pilots were not accepted socially or provided with equal opportunities. James was actively involved in several protests to provide equality for blacks in the military. In 1948 President Truman ordered the armed forces integrated.

In Korea, James flew 101 combat missions and earned his captain's bars. In 1956, by now a lieutenant colonel, James attended the Air Command and Staff College at Maxwell Air Force Base. His next assignment was the

United States Air Force in Washington, D.C., where he served in the Air Defense Division. For the next ten years he gained command experience in tactical fighter units at the squadron and wing levels.

Colonel James's next assignment was as deputy assistant secretary of defense. During this period in his career, he became one of the nation's most prolific public speakers. More promotions and responsibilities followed, and on September 1, 1975, General James received his fourth star, the first black ever to attain that rank. He also became commander in chief of the North American Air Defense Command.

Though he started life under circumstances that would have defeated lesser men, Chappy James pressed on. Why? Because he had the *right attitude*. He would quote his mother as saying, "Even though we are black and poor, you are one of God's children and . . . you can, *with the right attitude*, achieve high goals in life by developing character, working hard, and keeping your mind on your definite objective and continually striving for it with faith that it will be achieved."

Some years ago, my wife, Carolyn, and I met Marsha Christopher when Marsha helped us decorate our new home at the coast. Marsha is attractive and enthusiastic and always has a smile and a kind word for everybody. Carolyn and I liked her immediately, and soon we became close friends.

One evening Marsha called to tell us that on Saturday she was going into the hospital for a minor operation but that there was nothing to worry about. Earlier, we'd planned to have dinner that night with Marsha and her fiancé, Kit. But Marsha assured us the hospital visit wouldn't interfere with our plans, and that she'd see us Saturday night for dinner.

But when Saturday came, Marsha and Kit didn't meet us for dinner as planned. Concerned and puzzled, we called Marsha's office and the manager told us that during the operation it had been discovered that Marsha had cancer. They'd operated immediately, but were not successful: Marsha had incurable cancer.

Carolyn and I were stunned and grief-stricken. How could this beautiful young woman so full of life have cancer?

Though saddened, we decided we should go to the hospital to see Marsha. When we got there, she insisted we wait while she freshened up and put on some makeup. When she greeted us, she was just as happy and sweet and full of life as ever. She told us she was sure life had a great deal more to offer her. And as she talked, a strange thing happened: we found that, instead of our cheering Marsha up, she was cheering us up!

Some time later, she wrote a letter, which I feel sums up her attitude and her unconquerable will to live:

Dear George,

Please know how much your concern for me has meant. It's knowing people like you that has given me the courage and optimism to carry on. The story of your life is amazing. There is a time when I would have questioned it, but not anymore. Having cancer has given me an awareness of life that I cannot explain. It has brought Kit and me so close, and we never thought we could be closer. It has made me appreciate so many little things that I daily take for granted. It has brought me closer to my own self as well as to other people. It has convinced me that there are higher elements and forces in the world. Sadly enough, it's cancer that has brought me closer to God. The strange part in reading the story of your life is that I made an agreement with God, too. I agreed not to give up if he didn't. And I've never been a loser.

Much love,
Marsha

That was in 1976. Marsha is still very much alive. The doctor who pronounced her death sentence now calls her his "miracle girl," for Marsha is completely free of any trace of cancer. Did her attitude do it? I don't know for sure, but I do know it helped. *Had she not believed* she would beat cancer, I am convinced she would not be alive today.

ATTITUDE AND CAREER

If our goals are career goals, our attitudes are just as important as in our personal life.

I have seen people who were so well equipped educationally for the positions they held that on the basis of background, no one would ever predict failure. In fact, almost anyone would bet they would work their way to the stars. But they didn't. They didn't even get off the ground.

And I have seen people with very few educational credentials who have risen through the ranks and with each step have gained more and more knowledge than seemed possible.

A positive attitude does make the difference, and what a difference it makes! It is the difference between success and failure, between growth and being stunted. It opens the mind, expands it to search for new opportunities and to grow, to reach out, to touch other lives. It improves relations with superiors and subordinates and with fellow workers. Its constructive tone is what builds and expands any organization, whether it be a huge conglomerate or a garden club.

MOTIVATIONAL MEMO
Not only will a positive attitude change your life, but it will change your world as well.

A positive attitude in any endeavor is similar to a positive attitude in sports: The strongest, fastest, most gifted athlete can't win with a negative attitude. A positive attitude, however, will help him learn from his coaches and generate cooperation from his team members; it will inspire the entire team as well as those who watch the game.

ATTITUDE AND GOALS
The role of attitudes in achieving goals cannot be underestimated. Goals without a positive attitude are not goals at all. There is no sense in working toward them, for there is no way to reach them. Without a positive attitude there is no way to overcome stress and problems, no way to face temporary failure and to try again. Not only does a positive attitude point the direction in which one should strive, it also becomes the power plant that enables one to proceed in that direction.

The positive attitude says, "I will" and "I can," not "I'll see if I can make it." And when failure strikes, the positive attitude has a fall-back position from which it will try again and again, if necessary, to reach the goal through another route. But the fall-back position is never negative thinking; it is a reassessment, after having studied the failure to see if it offers a lesson.

Jesse Jackson, former director of Operation PUSH, believes a right attitude will help you achieve any goal. No matter how adverse your circumstances, how you react (your attitude) is up to you: "Even in the worst of situations, you still have the choice between the high road and the low road. It doesn't take money to buy character, integrity, and decency."

Wherever we look, we can find imperfection if that is what we are looking for. But imperfection has no reward; it gets us nowhere. The jeweler polishes away the imperfect parts of the stone until the smooth facets of the diamond sparkle brilliantly. It is the same stone that was covered by imperfections, but the goal of the jeweler was a sparkling diamond. He was inspired by a positive attitude, and he had faith in his ability to achieve his goal. Without the goal, the attitude, and the faith, he would have nothing but the rough-edged stone he started with.

A sculptor of Indian figures was asked how he could sculpt such accurate representations of Indians, and he replied that he cuts away everything that doesn't look like an Indian. This explanation, while a simplification, has the same ingredients as the illustration of the jeweler. Indeed, every goal we wish to reach has the same ingredients: positive attitude and faith.

Napoleon Hill and Clement W. Stone make two very important points in their best-selling book, *Success through a Positive Mental Attitude*: (1) You motivate by example, and (2) you can attract happiness. These are the products of a positive attitude, a positive way to look at things.

When I was a boy growing up in Kannapolis, North Carolina, I once heard our congressman, Hugh Alexander, tell this story:

A man was trying to put together a jigsaw puzzle of all the United States. After working on it, he became frustrated and suggested that his ten-year-old son give it a try.

Then later, to his astonishment, he found his son had completely assembled the puzzle. When he asked the boy how he did it, his son explained that the reverse side of the puzzle was a simple picture of a man: "See, Daddy, when you get the man together, you've got the country together."

We are given the opportunity to improve our surroundings, to motivate ourselves and others to achieve just a little bit more, to become a little bit better employee, employer, spouse, or parent, and we can do this by changing our attitudes.

TWENTY-TWO
Your Mind Is an Unlimited Source of Power

Too often we think of IQ as being the real factor that limits our use of the mind. If we have a high IQ, we are considered to have good mental powers for action; if our IQ is low, little can be expected of us.

This belief is false. The level of the IQ proves nothing about a person's ability to use the mind to solve problems and to get things done. A positive attitude conditions the mind to exercise and thus expand its ability to perform. But you have to do the exercising.

EXERCISING THE MIND
We often hear of instances where a person with a weak body has become a major sports contender. This is done via exercise, continuous and conscientious exercise of the muscles. O. J. Simpson, as you may recall, had rickety legs as

a child yet set many records as a running back for the Buffalo Bills football team.

The mind is very much like a muscle. If it's used and exercised, it will grow and expand its ability to perform just like the muscles of the body.

There is no way a healthy person who has not been exercising can go out and run a mile in six, eight, or even nine minutes. But if he exercises, if he works on it and keeps at it, he can build up his muscles and power and gradually accomplish his goal.

The same is true of your mind: Using it and exercising it with action will bring forth mental powers quite beyond normal expectations.

How does the athlete advance? He thinks winning thoughts. He wants to become an outstanding athlete. He visualizes himself being good at his sport. Then he follows the steps he must take to accomplish his goals. An example of an athlete using such visualizing powers is Franklin Jacobs, one of our country's premier high jumpers, though he is only five feet eight. Naturally, he says, "People have been asking me one basic question: How can a guy five-eight jump twenty-three and a half inches over his head? Quite honestly I never thought of myself as being small. Height to me is just a relative thing. When I approach that bar, I think I'm six-six."

How true this can be of the mind. We have specific steps to take in reaching certain objectives: What do we do first? And next? And just how is this done? Thinking this through and then actualizing these thoughts by mental exercise, by using our mind, is the way we grow.

If it is not used, the mind loses its ability to perform when we want it to and in the way we want it to.

HOW TO IMPROVE THE MIND

I believe that money problems in business are not our biggest problems. Our biggest problem is lack of ideas. Too many people are trying to find money for their business when they should be finding creative ways to overcome difficulties and turn problems around.

The same is true in one's personal world. Improving the mind is a step in the direction of turning things around to work in your favor. There are eight steps that I believe can improve your mind:

Believe you can do it. Believing something can be done puts your mind to work for you and helps you find ways to do it. Do not sell yourself short! Believe you can find solutions to personal problems. Believe you can find ways to make people like you. Believe you can find ways to buy that new home or that car. Believe you can succeed, and you will start in motion the greatest of all man's powers—the mind.

Think good things about your future. To get what you want, you must first think of helping the company, then the company will look after you.

Years ago there were some men driving spikes in cross ties on a railroad track when a train pulled up and somebody stepped out to speak with one of the workers. After the train moved on, one of the workmen said, "I cannot believe what just happened. The president of the railroad just stopped here to speak to you. How in the world do you know him?"

"Well," he said, "about thirty years ago we started to work on the same day doing the same job I am doing today."

"You mean to tell me that you both started off doing the same job! How come he is the president of the company and you are still out here driving spikes?"

The man answered, "I went to work for fifty cents an hour, and he went to work for the company."

Where business is concerned, people are not measured in inches, pounds, college degrees, or family background. They are measured instead by results and by the size of their thinking. How big we think determines the size of our accomplishments.

Use common sense. A common mistake is trying too hard to find a solution to a problem. Often we think a problem requires a difficult solution. Look for the simple ones first.

Stop thinking negatively. Thoughts can be controlled. Replace negative thoughts with positive ones. Use the negative thought only as a cue to replace it with a positive one. Golf great Tom Watson says this about negative thinking and how it can affect a person: "When you're thinking negatively, you're thinking about something you shouldn't do. In my case, I'd be thinking about where not to hit the ball. And the more I would think in this negative vein, the more likely I would be to hit the ball where it shouldn't go."

MOTIVATIONAL MEMO
Napoleon Hill's famous law of success states that "what the mind of man can conceive and believe, it can achieve."

Calm down. Many times people fail because they become so impatient they cannot think their problems through clearly. It is time then to back off and take a look at the situation. Come back to it after a period of meditation, relaxation, or perhaps even recreation. Most people have a certain period in the day when they are more productive mentally than at other times. You will know what your best time is. Leave the problem until then, when a relaxed mind may produce a quick and simple solution.

Stay alert and tuned in. One summer day, while lying on the beach, I was awakened by the rush of people running past me. Standing up, I saw a lifeguard swimming beyond the breakers to rescue a young girl in need of help. I had wondered earlier if the lifeguard could be counted on in case of emergency because he appeared to be almost asleep. So I asked him how, with all the noise, he could hear when someone needed help. "I am always listening for a cry of distress," he replied. "I can always distinguish it from other sounds if I stay tuned in."

So it is with the mind. We must stay alert and tuned in to what we are trying to accomplish and not be pulled off course by distractions along the way.

Forget mistakes. Dwelling on your mistakes does not change a thing. It keeps you facing in the wrong direction and wastes your time. Errors, mistakes, and struggles are a part of the learning process; but once they have served their purpose, they should be forgotten. Live for today and look forward to tomorrow; don't allow useless baggage to hold you down.

Open your mind to new ideas. Fixed routines can destroy initiative. They only pack your path down and make it harder. Become receptive to new ideas. Expose yourself to new things, new friends, new travels, new books, and new choices. Then you will enjoy new adventures and further expand your mind's ability to generate new ideas. That is what F. W. Woolworth did when he convinced his boss to have a ten-cent sale to reduce inventory. The idea worked so well that Woolworth decided to open a store and price items at a nickel and a dime. Would his boss supply capital? No, the idea was too risky; there would not be enough items to sell for five and ten cents. Later, his boss was to remark, "As far as I can figure, every word I used in turning Woolworth down cost me about a million dollars."

THE POWER OF THE MIND

Remember that the mind is similar to a computer. It does not question what you feed into it. It accepts everything, but it does use what you put into it to come up with ideas and solutions to your problems and to direct your action. If it is fed negative thoughts, that is what you are going to get back on the printout—just what you put in—negative advice. But positive input will result in positive output.

So sensitive is the mind to its conditioning that it can put a person in the hospital when he is not ill; it can cause a person to have a heart attack when he has a sound heart. But happily it can also bring rewards when properly conditioned.

Prentice-Hall, one of the country's largest reporting services for business, publishes a tax service. But it did not start out as a tax service. It was planned as a book. And the day the book was rolling off the press and through the bindery, the United States government passed new legislation outdating the book. Imagine the financial loss this could impose—a book that was out-of-date before it was even shipped from the bindery. No one would want it; it had no usefulness for anyone. Or did it? Could it be salvaged? The mind that had been fed positive thoughts was computing a solution to this dilemma, and a positive solution was coming forth. Cut off the bindings, punch the pages and insert them in a ring binder that could be updated with changes in the tax law as fast as they were issued. Forget the book. Sell a service. The problem became a very successful solution.

But on a personal level the same is possible. Think of my friend Bob Gilley. He was another of those persons who was condemned to die of a cancer. When it developed, depression came over him, negative thinking set in, and his resistance dropped sharply. But his "death sentence" shook him. He wanted to live. His attitude became passionate—"The only people who know when I will die are myself and God. Nobody else knows, and I will not let anyone forecast my death. I'll make that decision along with God." Into his mind computer he fed positive thoughts: "I will live. I will overcome my problem." There were times when he would become angry and curse his disease, demanding it to leave his body. He put positive slogans over his bedroom door and on the mirror where he shaved. He also fed his body the proper nourishment to help battle his disease. And he firmly believed in his mind, without any shadow of doubt, that he would live and conquer his disease. Today, Bob Gilley is a successful insurance executive and a very fine platform speaker. And he dedicates much of his time to helping others—all because he changed his attitude from one of defeat to one of winning, of overcoming adversity. His attitude triggered his mind to work for him, saving him from the "death sentence" his doctor had pronounced.

MIND AND MOTIVATION

When doctors believe a patient has an imaginary illness that does not call for normal medication, a placebo may be prescribed. This is usually a sugar-coated pill that has no effect whatever on the patient except that the patient thinks it does. And often the patient will feel he is cured of his problem after taking the placebo.

The placebo experiment has been tried on people in connection with studies of the mind, and the results are quite amazing. No sugar-coated pill was used, but instead a teacher was told that her students had very high IQ's when in reality she was working with below-average children. But she treated them as if they were very bright children. As a result, she was more inspiring and more enthusiastic. And the students responded with amazing results. They became top learners, making high marks just because someone thought they were bright and capable. They were responding to having positive teaching methods to exercise their minds. The teacher read the IQ's written in after the name of each child—125, 130, 138, 140, and 165. A room of geniuses, she thought, and she treated them as such. Not until after the end of the school year did she learn that the numbers after their names were really their locker numbers.

So, we have it within ourselves to use the mind as a motivating force in dealing with ourselves and those with whom we come in contact. Although we compared the mind to a computer, it can function in ways a computer never can, for it humanizes our own behavior and our behavior toward others.

TWENTY-THREE
Explore the Unknown

When we think of exploring the unknown, we usually think of Columbus, who ventured forth on new and uncharted seas, not knowing what lay ahead. There was a certain high quality of courage and excitement about this. As a result, a hero was born.

Today, we also think of the astronauts shooting skyward at speeds that are impossible to comprehend, venturing forth on new and uncharted orbits and not knowing what lies ahead. Courage and excitement still abound. Again, present-day heroes are born.

Columbus and the astronauts have something in common—the ability to explore the unknown. Their desire to explore the unknown gave them the faith that the unknown could not destroy them, faith that they would succeed in reaching their goals, faith in those who built their vehicles, who designed their instruments of navigation, and who worked to support their explorations.

YOU AND THE UNKNOWN

We are not unlike Columbus and the astronauts. As babies, we come into this world not knowing what lies ahead. We must have blind faith in our parents to nourish, clothe, and protect us. Later we recognize faith in parents and our teachers to guide us to that point where we have enough faith in ourselves to stand alone.

· Yet every day we are still facing the unknown—something new, something we cannot predict with 100 percent certainty.

In fact, from this very moment onward, we face the unknown. Surely we know the sun will rise tomorrow and the next day and the next. We know that night follows day and that spring will follow winter, for it always has. But of things outside the solar system we really know little for certain. Weather forecasts to the contrary, we won't really know until tomorrow what the weather will be, and we won't know until it arrives what kind of spring we will have: Wet? Cold? Early? No one knows when the next hurricane will strike or when the next earthquake will wreak its damage, or how severe these disasters will be.

THE CHALLENGE OF THE UNKNOWN

The unknown is a challenge, much as a problem is a challenge. It presents us with new opportunities for self-expression, for helping others, for reaching our goals, for exercising our mind, and for using our talents.

While we enjoy studying the past as history, there is little challenge in the future if we know what is going to happen. The same old routine day after day becomes boring with no opportunities for growth and development. It would prevent the mind from finding the solutions to problems, new inventions, and new ways of thinking and expressing.

The key to the unknown is *change*. Our entire world—nature and humanity—is in a constant state of unrest. Our ideas are constantly changing; so are our problems and our priorities. Change is the very essence of the spirit of adventure. It has been well said that the only constant thing in life (and the only sure thing) is change. We can depend on it, we can predict it, and we can watch it happen.

Imagine the dullness of life if, for instance, a baby were always a baby. Or if instead of our beautiful forests, the trees were always seedlings. Or if our problems were precisely the same problems. Things would be just as dull if our mind was never to expand. There would be no spirit of adventure, no opportunities for helping others, no opportunities to help ourselves.

Were there no change, having goals would be meaningless, focusing would be an empty exercise, and no progress could be measured.

We have to explore; the creative mind has to move out and expand. Exploring is essential not only for our businesses and professions but also for our career and our personal life. It is easy to become lodged in a rut; that is the beginning of the end for many individuals and businesses. There is no action in a rut, no opportunity to explore and grow, no excitement, no adventure, no opportunity to serve. We need these activities to make life meaningful.

GOALS AND THE UNKNOWN

Setting a goal is establishing an objective that does not exist at the moment, else it would not be a new goal. Reaching the goal takes a certain amount of time, depending on what the goal is and the conditions for reaching it. So reaching your goal is seeking to change something from the present state, where you start, to a future state, where your goal is reached. Since the future is the unknown, the unknown becomes the opportunity—the challenge.

All goals are set within a context of the unknown, the area where things are happening. We should prepare ourselves to work toward improving ourselves so we can participate fully in challenging the unknown. This we can do, and successfully, if we develop confidence in our abilities.

MOTIVATIONAL MEMO
The motivated person explores the unknown every day, by having, as Robert Frost put it, "the courage to act on limited knowledge and insufficient evidence."

TAKING RISKS WITH THE UNKNOWN

So life is a risk; we don't know what is going to happen from this moment onward, but we have to be prepared to meet it. We have the choice of facing life with its uncertainties or of doing nothing and letting death claim our present self. Happily, most of us choose life—risk. We believe in our abilities to control some of the changes in life and to work to reach our goals. This type of risk does not mean flinging caution to the winds and abandoning common sense, good judgment, and personal morality. It is calculated risk, based on planning and preparation.

First obtain all the facts you can, get advice and input from people who you know can be helpful, and try to minimize as much as possible the obvious risk involved. Your judgment on what to do becomes your calculated risk. If a person takes his hard-earned money and invests without investigating, he is asking for trouble.

The man of wisdom will investigate first to minimize his risk.

And even after calculated risk is evaluated, hard work is required, for there is no regard without work. Work makes things happen and overcomes the day-to-day problems and the bigger ones that pop up along the way.

THE FUTURE

There is something about the future that challenges everyone. We want things to be better, and most of us have faith that things will be better. If we decry the present and the past because of their problems, we still have faith that the future can improve. There is a certain amount of optimism for the future even among those who are disenchanted with life. Faith that things will be good, or better, has to involve a look at ourselves, for we are the ones who will have to act if life is going to improve.

All this was perhaps best expressed by King George VI to his people during some dark moments following World War II:

> I said to the man who stands at the Gate of the Year, "Give me light that I may tread safely into the unknown." And he replied, "Step into the darkness, put your hands into the hand of God, and that will be better to you than a light and safer than a known way."

TWENTY-FOUR
Love Yourself and Others

It is generally accepted that the statement of St. Paul in his first letter to the Corinthians, chapter 13, is the greatest statement about love that has ever been made. Here translators have used the word *charity* as a synonym for love, and the chapter ends with these words: "And now abideth faith, hope, charity [love], these three; but the greatest of these is charity [love]."

The entire chapter describes the power of love. In fact, it can be a bit humbling to read this chapter and then to realize how we fail to grasp its power and how little we use it.

One person who does know the power of love is Johnny Cash. Cash is convinced it was the power of love that saved him from a ten-year nightmare of drug abuse.

Cash had started using amphetamines and other drugs to fight off the fatigue and loneliness of the concert tour. Used occasionally at first, the drugs became a monkey on his back. His marriage broke up; he began to miss concert days and to spend more nights behind bars, locked up for reckless behavior while under the influence of drugs and alcohol.

It was one such overnight stop in the La-Fayette, Georgia, jail that brought Cash's slide to an abrupt halt. When Sheriff Ralph Jones freed Johnny the next morning, he gave him back his pills, but when he did so, he told the singer: "I've watched you on television and listened to you on the radio; we've got your albums of hymns. We're probably the two best fans you ever had.

"It broke my heart when they brought you in here last night. I left the jail and went home to my wife and told her I had just locked up Johnny Cash. I almost wanted to resign and just walk out because it was such a heartbreaking thing for me. Here, take your pills and get out of here. Do with your life whatever you want to. Just remember, you've got the free will to either kill yourself or save your life."

It was that talk straight from the heart that snapped Johnny Cash out of it. He began a month-long fight to withdraw from his drug habit. It was pure agony, but Cash had help. As he says, "I did it by humbling myself like a child, admitting that I couldn't do it alone and that I needed my friends and loved ones and God."

THE ROLE OF HAPPINESS
We talk a great deal about happiness, using the word quite loosely, thinking that it means everything will go just the way we want it to go—no problems at all.

But this is not so. In describing love, St. Paul did not say there would be no problems, that there would be no confrontations with those who disagree with you. But he did say that love was the most important thing.

If we agree that love is the key to happiness, from Paul's description of love we have to assume that happiness is a psychological state, one that is deeply concerned with the well-being of yourself and others. It does not emphasize material wealth but instead spiritual and psychological satisfaction.

This kind of satisfaction does not eliminate problems, grief, and pain. But it does give one the spiritual fortitude to withstand grief and pain, and it does present problems as a challenge.

Grief and pain remind us of the artist's canvas. The backdrop may be dark, but the bright colors stand out against the dark background with greater brilliance than if the background were bright and sparkling. Still, this does not harm the picture; in fact, it enhances it. And we feel uplifted with the artist's rendition.

So it is with happiness. The peak moments of life mean little when every minute is a peak moment. But painted against the other moments in life when one is called to build where there has been destruction, to bring comfort where grief and sorrow have intruded, to share support where support was lacking—these are the instances that make the peak moments stand out, that make happiness the true reflection of love.

LOVE OF SELF

A rereading of St. Paul's famous chapter inspires us to believe that to love our fellowman we must first love ourselves. Self-esteem is where it all begins. If we have no love for ourselves, we will have no personal goals, no standards against which to measure ourselves, nothing to show others that we really care.

George Bernard Shaw said, "We have no more right to consume happiness without producing it than to consume wealth without producing it." In other words, each one of us is responsible for producing happiness wherever it may be—in ourselves and in others. We cannot partake of it if we are not able to bring happiness about.

Personal happiness, based on St. Paul's letter

to the Corinthians, helps us to grab for those problems that are challenges for us to solve, helps us win over grief and pain, and makes us show concern for our fellowmen.

There is no way we can escape giving a top priority to loving ourselves. Until we do, we have nothing to give away.

Furthermore, if we want to be loved by others, we first have to deserve the privilege of being loved. This begins with attention to ourselves, making certain that we, as God's children, care enough about ourselves to honor God in being examples of the love He has shown.

MOTIVATIONAL MEMO
Love has no value unless it is shared.

Even St. Paul recognized this when he pointed out that we have to start with ourselves: no envy, but patience and kindness; no egotism, no joy in seeing others wronged, no selfishness, and no time for evil thoughts.

It is tempting to think of self-esteem as selfishness, but indeed it is not. We are here by the grace of God, and as a gift of God we have an obligation to care for ourselves as caring for God's property, which is what we really are doing. The way we treat ourselves is indicative of how much we care for God. And from the way we treat ourselves flows the love to others.

LOVE AND MOTIVATION

"What has love got to do with motivation?" you may ask.

The goal of motivation is to inspire yourself and others to action, action you can be proud of, action that is based on truth and love.

Over and over we are told that example is the key to leadership. If we want people to do something for us, we must inspire them by example. In short, we get what we give. If we give hatred, we receive hatred; if we give impatience, we receive impatience; if we give love, we receive love.

Love is not love when it is cooped up; it is not a source of power until you give it away. In other words, love is action. It motivates, just as the explosion in a gasoline engine motivates the engine to action. There is nothing conditional about it. The gasoline engine causes nothing but frustration when the explosion is not complete; so does love when it is conditional. Love must come first, then action will follow.

THE RISKS OF LOVE

Are there any risks in loving others? Yes, there can be. The greatest is perhaps the risk of being misunderstood. Some may think you have ulterior motives, hopes of bringing some special good to yourself by being attentive to the needs of others. But in spite of this and other risks, love has a way of taking care of such risks.

A young woman who was born with a physical defect developed a strong dislike for acts of kindness others showed her. She interpreted them as pity. But she had great talents that she shared with others, and she did not think it inconsistent when she extended special kindness to others during their times of emergency and peril. Quite suddenly one day she was the victim of a traumatic experience, and neighbors and friends came to her aid. She adamantly refused to accept the expressions of love and compassion her neighbors were bringing her. Then it was pointed out that others were doing only what she had done for them, emulating her example. Soon love itself cured the risk love had taken, and an unhealthy situation was resolved.

There are other risks in love, but love will cure them in love's own time, providing love is constant. Loving one day and not loving the next is a certain way to stamp "opportunism" on the act. Constant love, however, will overcome all risks that arise, for as we have said, love's expression of life is in giving itself away.

LOVE AND FORGIVENESS

One of the greatest expressions of love is forgiveness, but often forgiving is very difficult.

When an action done by another person is misinterpreted, emotions may be deep-rooted. This is especially true if one has allowed thoughts of the act to persist for a long time. Hatred and distrust are common by-products of such thoughts, and far too frequently there is a desire for revenge, to get even with those who committed the act. But this only leads to further distrust and desire for revenge on both sides. Distrust and hatred spawn their own like, but in even greater degree.

Forgiveness takes guts! It takes guts whether you are the one asking for forgiveness or the one forgiving. And it takes very special guts when you forgive someone who does not respond positively to your forgiving.

But forgiving is an act of love. Accordingly, forgiveness, like love, will work to heal the relationship between persons even though time may be required.

Furthermore, forgiveness must be complete, else there is no forgiveness. Sometimes we can almost forgive another, but not quite. When this happens, there is progress, but no true forgiveness until one is ready to forgive completely and never again allow the reason for the breach to have any effect on one's behavior.

Corrie ten Boom, in her book *The Hiding Place*, tells of seeing years later the woman who had been responsible for the death of her sister in the Nazi prison camp. What a challenge that was for one to forgive! But she did, and as a result the life of the woman was dramatically changed for the good. This took guts, real guts. But it was love working its way through forgiveness to the complete restoration of a person's life.

Richard Garrett, a nineteenth-century poet, expressed it this way:

> Joy to forgive, and joy to be forgiven
> Hang level in the balance of love.

A KERNEL OF LOVE . . .
One kernel of corn will become one stalk of corn when planted. This one stalk will bear probably two ears of corn, each of which will yield approximately 200 kernels. And these kernels will become 400 stalks of corn, each of which will have a couple of new ears of corn with a total of 400 kernels. Imagine, if you will, a total of 160,000 kernels from one ear that you started with just one season ago! That is called geometric progression.

We see many other examples of geometric progression around us all the time. The human population explosion is such an example. Another is the germ that enters a body to develop a cold. It multiplies rapidly and so do its offspring and their offspring. Soon we have a patient with a cold. Then antibodies start to build up to counteract the cold germs. Both the cold germs and the antibodies increase geometrically.

But there is something else that expands geometrically, something whose expansion we often overlook. I am speaking about love. It is a fact that the more you give away, the more you have. It really does come back to you in more ways than you ever dreamed when you extend love to another person. Not only does love do nothing when it is cooped up, it has no purpose until it is given away. And when it is given away, it rebounds in giant quantities and in many different forms.

Love is indeed the greatest motivating force known to mankind, and it is born out of faith in God, the source of all love.

TWENTY-FIVE
The Strongest Force Known

I believe without any doubt whatsoever that *faith* is the strongest force known. When I say faith, I mean faith in God, faith in others, faith in yourself, and faith in our country. I also believe that faith is the prime motivator of man. The firmness of my belief has convinced me that every problem has a solution if this great source of power will only be used. Faith does not make things happen automatically; we have to work for the rewards that faith has in store for us.

WHAT IS FAITH?
In many ways faith is intangible. We see its results, and we accept things by faith.

You have faith in your automobile. You drive it to work, on vacation, and to emergencies. You have confidence that it will get you where you want to go. If you take care of your automobile, keep it serviced, and do not abuse it, then you can count on many miles of trustworthy use.

You trust your home for shelter, and you trust electricity to keep your refrigerator running, or you would not invest in frozen food.

You believe in all these tangible things. You trust them and have confidence in them, and you should. But you should have more faith in the important things in life—faith in God, in other people, in yourself, and in our country. Faith in God will give you strength of purpose, faith in people will give you strength of character, and faith in yourself will give you hope and concern for the world.

Faith is a source of strength from within that favors no race. It binds no person to remain in poverty because he was born to poverty, it restores health when all else fails, it heals the wounds of sorrow. And faith is the one thing that eliminates fear. Fear is real—it is one of the strongest forces known—but faith is stronger. Faith will always overcome fear.

Loyalty, honesty, sincerity, trust, confidence, and unquestioning belief all mean faith. Faith tells us we must have a purpose in life, that life can be meaningful, and that all our efforts need not be in vain. Faith—the greatest weapon against worry, greed, jealousy, envy, hatred, revenge, doubt, and fear.

Faith in God. I have complete faith that God has a plan for me, and that He will reward me if I will work to do what is right. He has promised that if I am ever tempted or in danger, He will provide me with a way of escape.

And my contact with God is through prayer. I am not one of those who believe that prayers should be formal and always on bended knee. I reach God in prayer wherever I am, regardless of what I am doing—in the shower, driving, jogging, in the office, or visiting with friends and business associates. I take my problems to God with complete faith that He will give me the right answers, although they may not be the ones I had been hoping and looking for. But I do have absolute faith that God will give a solution for my problems if I will do my day-to-day work toward finding that solution, and if I will constantly strive to recognize God as my Provider. I have never been let down or disappointed, although there have been times when, if I had not had faith, I would have wondered if things would really turn out all right. I also believe there has to be a motivation on my part to get a response from God. He doesn't expect me to sit around and do nothing. He supplies the harvest, but He expects me to do the cultivating.

Eyra Dell Petrea, who lives in Concord, North Carolina, is a living testament to the power of faith in God, for it is that faith that keeps Eyra Dell going despite an almost unbelievable series of personal tragedies.

She has been paralyzed three times. She has had to learn to walk seven times. She is a diabetic. She has cataracts in both eyes. In a single year, both her hands, her shoulder, and her hip were broken.

Her left hand and her face are the only parts of her body that can distinguish between hot and cold, or wet and dry. She cannot walk without the aid of crutches. Walking with her crutches is dangerous for her because a blood clot in her hip affects her muscles, causing her to bend forward, which makes it easy to fall.

She has had all her teeth knocked out. In the past twenty-six years, she has spent 90 percent of her time in bed. She has had some sixty operations. Her ribs have been broken several times.

Despite all of this suffering, Eyra Dell is happy to be alive and actually considers her misfortunes blessings in disguise. It is her faith in God, she says, that gives her the strength to look at the world the way she does. She says her troubles give her the ability to "witness to someone who is hurting and to smile with them. God is trying to make me more like Him in showing love to others."

Faith in People. Why should we have faith in

other people? Because they, too, are God's children, God's property. We manifest such faith by love. True, there are times when we are disappointed in others even as they are disappointed in us, but unless others can be accepted by faith, we cannot be either. In spite of scandals, wars, and crime, I have faith in the basic goodness of people.

Where scandals, wars, and crime have occurred, there is almost always a history of people not wanting to become involved, of people taking no action in the affairs of men. Indifference is an evil as great as a major crime because it festers and infects the goodness of people.

MOTIVATIONAL MEMO
There is no stronger force known to mankind than for a human being to get down on his knees and ask God for guidance.

I like to imagine that God has put me on earth so I will have an opportunity to express His teachings in my relationship with other people. It is interesting to note, too, that so much of the Bible concerns people and an individual's relationship with people. Unless I have faith in others (even though I may be disappointed from time to time), I would have no alternative except a negative attitude toward others, and negative attitudes produce no good and are counter to God's commands.

In dealing with others, one of the most powerful acts of love is forgiveness, and faith is the very support of forgiveness.

Faith in Self. Courage and self-confidence do not exist unless one has faith in oneself. And faith in oneself is a by-product of faith in God. Far too often we see people who will not, or cannot, act because they do not dare. Fright, uncertainty, and lack of self-confidence prohibit their taking charge of themselves when action is required. How pitiful these cases are! They are even more pitiful when those involved have failed to realize that they can overcome the problems they have. Realizing there is a greater Power than oneself to help in times of need, and believing in that Power to do right by you, can cancel all feelings of insufficiency and lack of self-confidence. The cure is waiting for you to grasp it and be on your way with a steadfastness that puts spirit into action.

Faith in Country. At times it becomes very discouraging to read the newspapers or listen to the news, for crime, disobedience, and massive problems are constantly headlined. Stories about good seldom become news at all.

But we have to have faith in our country. If we don't, life is not worth living here. Our country has been good to us. When we look back over the years, it is surprising how much has been achieved since the early settlers carved a home out of the wilderness. Almost all activities literally astound me when I consider what has been accomplished. Think, for instance, of our transportation facilities, of our methods of distributing food and household necessities throughout our land, of the housing that has been constructed in two hundred years, of the advances of medical science and the eradication of disease, of the progress made in our educational systems, of the great resources that have made it possible for industry to expand, of the communications systems that we feel we could not endure without. I could go on and on.

Sure we have problems. But there have always been problems. The diaries of early settlers tell of starvation and death, of disease and lack of clothing, of lack of shelter and communications, of floods and the perils of the sea and storms. The point to which we have arrived today in the control and solution of these problems has been achieved only because they were accepted as challenges, and the "faith of our fathers" helped provide answers to these problems. Today we have new problems. Thank God we still have problems to challenge us. And I believe God will provide us with an answer to these problems if we, like our forefathers, will work to find His solution.

In short, faith in God, in others, in ourselves, and in our country are all interrelated. Omit one, and the others fall apart, but keep them all together, and we can live a life of faith with works. The late George Mardikian, an Armenian immigrant who arrived in this country with neither money nor a word of English, struggled up through a series of menial jobs to become one of the country's leading restaurateurs. Here is his testimony to what faith can do: "That July morning when I first saw the Statue of Liberty from the deck of the immigrant steamer, it was like suddenly hearing a hymn of hope. The priceless thing America has given me has nothing to do with money or fame. . . . I call it the dignity of being an American. Many fine young Americans have a chance to be something. . . . Have faith in yourself, faith in your country, and foremost, faith in Almighty God. Back this up with hard work and nothing can stop you."

HOW TO PREPARE YOUR MIND FOR FAITH

I have found these four steps very helpful in preparing my mind for faith:

—*Think positively.* Cleanse your mind of all negative thoughts such as fear, greed, jealousy, hatred, doubt, and worry. The power of faith will move in and take action only when the mind has been cleared of all negative thoughts.

—*Have self-respect.* Believe in yourself. You are a child of God, and you are important to Him. So consider yourself important. If you think of yourself as a doormat, people will walk all over you.

—*Forget failure.* Consider defeat only as temporary and accept it as inspiration for greater effort, and continue to believe you will succeed. Considering failure as failure is true failure.

—*Trust in God.* Without God you have nothing. With God, you have everything within your grasp.

DEMONSTRATIONS OF FAITH

Once we have prepared our minds for faith, we must demonstrate our faith with the proper motivation. There are many ways, but I present the following three to you as being basic:

—*You must have a purpose.* You need something toward which to work, a goal or objective. Decide on your goals and objectives, then focus on your achievement of them.

—*You must be willing to take a chance.* There is always a certain amount of risk involved in faith, but without faith, nothing is accomplished.

—*You must take action*. Faith is not a substitute for work. Faith is not laziness. But faith backed by action knows no fear and denies all despair. Faith is not an accident nor is it luck. Success is not an accident nor is it luck. Success is the result of faith and hard work.

Again, let me say that I believe without reservation that faith is the strongest force known. And it is there for all to tap. No goal in life will materialize without being blessed with the goodness of faith.

UNIT
VI
MOTIVATING YOURSELF INTO ACTION

TWENTY-SIX
Set and Reach Your Personal Goals

The purpose of motivation is to get *action*—not just a random action but specific action. The willingness to act on your ideas is at least as important as the ideas themselves. I remember making a presentation to a client several years ago. His name was Charles Harbottle, and he was (and still is) one of the leaders in the private school industry. After we finished our discussion, Charles said, "George, you've got a deal."

But then Charles added, "George, there's nothing in your proposal that I haven't thought of, nothing that I haven't seen tried before. But George, the difference is, *I know you'll do it.*" In other words, I hadn't come up with any new, world-beating ideas, and Charles knew that I had far less experience than he did. But the big difference was, as Charles put it, "You have the *motivation* to get the job done."

Successful people often get motivated by setting goals. If you want to be successful, you need to know where you are going.

Before the 1980 Olympics, Eric Heiden knew where he was going. When asked what his goal was, he said: "I'm shooting for five gold medals." Heiden, you may recall, won those five medals.

George P. Kneeland, chief executive of the giant St. Regis Paper Company, realizes the value of a sense of personal direction. The most important thing, he says, in his rise from a sixty-five-dollar-a-month job in the mail room to chief executive officer was, "knowing where I wanted to go. So much time is wasted when you don't know what it is you want out of life."

The person who wishes to get ahead will set up certain goals he wishes to reach, goals that he will work toward as he develops his talents. Therefore, he needs a plan.

Plans are to one's personal life what blueprints are to the contractor building a house. Without blueprints there is no shape, and the contractor would have no idea what materials would be required, how many people would be needed to complete the work, or how fast the building would have to be constructed to complete it on schedule.

We, too, need some kind of blueprint, something that can be a plan of action to help us develop our talents in the direction of our specific goals.

In our organization we put so much emphasis on the matter of personal goals that we seek to hire only those who are goal-oriented. We feel that no company can grow and expand without goal-oriented employees. All of our executives, for example, make a list of annual goals. At year's end, we measure their performance against those goals and set new goals for the coming year.

Different people have different goals, but the goals should be attainable. They should also be *your* goals—not goals that someone else wishes you to reach.

Among my acquaintances, almost without exception, those who have been successful in their personal lives as well as in their professional lives have told me that the secret of their success was goal setting. Goals give purpose and direction. They are the bull's-eye of the target of life. They are the guts of the success system. Without them there is no purpose, no growth, no action.

ESTABLISHING PERSONAL GOALS
The important thing, then, is to establish goals you feel in your heart you want to achieve to bring happiness to yourself and to others. (People can be your goal, too, because the

object of goal-setting is to help others, not just to make money.) Whether you want to become an outstanding student, a better wife or husband, or a business success, you first need to decide what your long-range goals are, and what it will take in time, effort, and money to reach them. It might require a number of years to obtain the necessary education to fulfill your objectives for certain professions; you must figure this in. In certain areas of business you may be required to work as an apprentice before obtaining the necessary background to reach your goals; all this must be figured in.

There is a definite technique to setting goals. First of all, they must not in any way violate the laws of God or man. Second, as we have already said, they must be attainable. Over the long range there is no point in reaching for something you know is utterly impossible; yet you should recognize that goals will help you attain many of the things you never thought were possible. Furthermore, if one of your goals pertains to your job, which you dislike, try to improve your attitude and give of yourself 100 percent. If you still go unnoticed, then find a new job before setting that goal, a job that promises to be fulfilling and one with a future for you. Next, you should set specific and clearly defined goals that you wish to achieve in five, ten, or twenty years from now.

Why is the timing so important? Because this enables you to use the "divide and conquer" technique. For instance, you may have a non-career goal of reading twelve books a year, as I do. This means you must average one a month. I have another goal of jogging a thousand miles a year. This means I should average about twenty miles a week to reach that goal. One of your goals may be to diet and lose forty pounds. It would not be wise to lose that all at once, but your doctor may advise losing it over eighteen months. You know then that you should average a little over two pounds a month.

Don't underestimate the "divide and conquer" method. It makes reaching goals much easier and provides excellent opportunities to check on your progress periodically.

A periodic check is very important. Then you know whether you are progressing on schedule or whether your timing should be reevaluated. We all like encouragement from time to time, and reviewing progress and finding that we are on schedule is good for our morale. But if we are off schedule or way ahead of schedule, it is to our advantage to know this as early as possible so we can change our method of action or timing.

At certain points of accomplishment it is good to reward yourself or celebrate the occasion in some way. Reaching goals is not always easy; in fact, it shouldn't be. It is an occasion for stretching a bit! That is why celebrating progress is important.

SETBACKS AND OBSTACLES

Regardless of how careful your planning may be, it is possible that your goal plan will not work perfectly. Things happen that we cannot foresee. Circumstances change. Obstacles arise from time to time, often without warning.

Crises are opportunities, and how you seize these opportunities is up to you. Like the problems we have discussed, crises are often blessings in disguise. So while you should have a goal plan against which to measure success and progress, you should always remain flexible—loose—so you can make modifications in your plan as circumstances require. For good reason your goal plan may have to be stretched out or even speeded up. Perhaps some other factor may suggest advantageous changes. Be prepared to seize the opportunity by being relaxed and flexible.

The great military strategists have always had a contingency plan in case their battle plans, for some reason, did not work out. The backup plan was really an alternative to be used to circumvent an obstacle. In goal planning, backup plans are also useful insofar as we are able to predict what obstacles may come before us. If your goal is to own a house, and this becomes impossible, you should have given some advance thought to alternatives. What are your options?

MOTIVATIONAL MEMO
By the yard it's hard, but by the inch it's a cinch.

However, there is a certain danger in making too firm a backup plan too far in advance. Reaching a goal should involve constant effort, and there is danger that one may become lulled into a safer route if the contingency plan seems easier. Use your backup plan only when you know the main plan will not work best for you. Let wisdom be your guide; don't be misled by wishful thinking.

TIMING
Success in reaching your goals has much to do with timing. Far too often we tend to put off setting goals and starting the program that will lead to their achievement. The time is *now*, right now. Goals are much too important to postpone. Your future depends on them. Your family depends on them for its happiness. Your success with friends and business acquaintances depends on your reaching them. Don't put them off. Take time right now to consider

what your goals should be and map out steps to achieve them.

How long it takes you to reach your goals depends on how high you set them and on how hard you are willing to work to reach them. Realism, patience, and faith work together to help you, but even so, the road will not always be easy. Nevertheless, it can be rewarding, exciting, and often fun if you will stick to your plan and celebrate your progress from time to time.

Be alert to the need to set new goals. Keep moving constantly and do not allow yourself to become discouraged or slowed down. Don't consult negative thinkers—they will discourage you and tell you it can't be done. If you need to ask advice, seek it from believers, those who have reached their goals successfully.

A GOAL-SETTING CHECKLIST

The pilot of our company plane has a checklist he goes through before he takes off. Living successfully should have a checklist, too, a checklist of long-range and short-range goals. I pass on to you my goal-setting checklist, which has been most useful in helping me reach many goals:

> —Set specific goals in all areas of personal and business life.
> —Reserve quiet time for consideration and formulation of goals. *Write them down.*

—Do your own thinking. You are responsible for your own destiny, for the achievement of your goals. If you need advice, ask believers!

—Face up to obstacles. Define the problem, identify alternatives; then pick a solution and use it. But keep moving.

—Goals should allow you to take action, to do something about achieving what you want in life rather than just letting things happen.

—Short-range goals make the accomplishment of long-range goals easier.

—Set goal priorities. Some goals are obviously more important than others.

—Review your goals often. Check your progress. Ask yourself, How realistic are my goals? Should I reach higher? Should I aim lower? Are they still valid in the light of experience? Have I been trying my best?

—Have a backup plan if need be, but don't let it distract you from your main goal just because it may be easier.

—Be a decision maker. Pick a goal route and take it. *Now.*

—Be alert to opportunities of turning problems you encounter along the way into opportunities.

YOUR BEST SELF
Your best self should be the inspiration for your goals. Visualize yourself as the person you wish to be. Burn that picture into your mind. Keep it before you. Then consider what you have to do to bring that image of your best self into what you want it to be. That will determine what your goals should be. Goals are steps toward the successful development of your best self.

TWENTY-SEVEN
Become a Self-Starter

It was not so long ago that the driver of an automobile had to hand-crank the engine of his car before it would start. This was often a hard job, especially if the engine was cold. Furthermore, it was not always safe, and some drivers sprained their arms while trying to start their engine by cranking.

Then along came the automatic engine ignition—faster, safer, easy, and efficient. And soon the old-fashioned hand cranks were no more.

It was not many years before automation seemed to be everywhere. Along came automatic transmissions, refrigerators and defrosters, oven cleaners, water pumps, lights that would turn on automatically as darkness increased, automatic pilots for airplanes, automatic smoke alarms, and many, many more automated inventions—all designed for increased efficiency.

The day of the automatic mechanism had arrived. Self-starting mechanisms would displace the slower, more cumbersome, and less efficient models.

But what about people? Have they become automated? They certainly have, at least some of them. They are called "self-starters," and they outstrip the other models who have to be coaxed into action before they will move. The day of the self-starter is at hand, when people independently and automatically will get up and move to accomplish their goals.

Are you a self-starter, or do you wait around for someone to crank your engine?

PRIMING YOUR OWN PUMP

When hand pumps were used by families to obtain well water, a pail of water was kept nearby to pour into the pump to prime it before it would work. Priming the pump started the action.

Who primes your pump?

The self-starter primes his own pump. He wakes with excitement and expectancy thinking that "today will be a great day." He has his goals clearly in mind, he focuses on the achievement of his goals, he has a plan to reach them, and his positive attitude strengthens his determination to meet every problem with success. He fills his mind with good thoughts that include what he can do for others as well as for himself. His life is a dream with muscle. Life is an opportunity not to be wasted, and the self-starter is there to take advantage of every opportunity.

Just how does the self-starter go forward each day with this exhilarating approach to life? For him it is simple. He has self-confidence.

SELF-CONFIDENCE AND MOTIVATION

Self-confidence is crucial to motivation. But self-confidence comes by way of self-analysis and a constant effort to develop your abilities to such an extent that you have complete assurance you can do whatever you desire. Self-confidence is not ego; it is a humble analysis that taps inner power and gives one courage to act. The self-starter knows his pluses and minuses, and he constantly turns his minuses into pluses. He is unafraid to act even though risk is involved, for he recognizes that action is a learning process.

Time is not wasted; each moment is dedicated to something constructive, something with meaning. Moments of prayer and meditation are as important to his growth as moments of recreation and wonderment. His books and friends add meaning to his goals. The "great day" he envisioned upon arising is a "great day" all day because he makes it so. His weather report is not "partly cloudy," it is "partly sunny." His goals are not the end; they are but stepping-stones to greater ones.

MOTIVATIONAL MEMO

The motivated man or woman must have that personal quality of *initiative,* that inner urge that prods him or her from a position of inertia to *movement, change, action.*

In our organization the people who get ahead are the self-starters. We have to have them. We cannot spend our time and energy every day having to encourage and motivate each person who works for us. We don't push them up; they pull themselves up.

Self-confidence and motivation combine for positive action, and positive action is the only action the self-starter knows.

I have been impressed with the way people in the world of sports have worked to arrive at championship levels—their goals. Take Bruce Jenner, for instance. He sacrificed three years of his life preparing for the 1976 Olympics. He had no coach prodding him but worked just as hard as if he had one. He had to rely on motivation to carry him to his goals. But he believed in himself, and he knew that the decathlon was within his grasp if he would work for it. And he won.

Yogi Berra was another who had no time for defeat. People ridiculed him when he joined the Yankees in 1947 because he was short and heavy. One time he hit an umpire while attempting to throw out a runner at second base. But he never gave up; he was determined to reach his goals. He was a self-starter, and he worked at it. He studied rival hitting in order to help his pitcher. He stayed after practice, improving his hitting. What was his payoff? He hit 358 homers and set fourteen World Series records that still stand. He also was the American League's Most Valuable Player three times. No one did it for him; he was his own starter and he had the self-confidence and the motivation needed to reach his goals.

Yet another example from the world of sports is tennis great Billie Jean King. Here's what she said: "I'm gonna prove that motivation is more important than anything, provided you're healthy. Winning matches depends on how much you care. Some players are influenced by the way the public perceives them. But I'm not gonna let anyone undermine me. No way. People think when you reach thirty you're through. They look at the big three-oh and figure it's all over.

Well, I'll tell you something. I'm gonna be moving a whole lot faster when I'm sixty-five than people who are thirty and think that way."

What a philosophy! What a person! What a testimony for motivation!

And here is another of her secrets: "I never thought of the finish line. I thought beyond it, so when I hit the finish line I was still reaching out. I'll bet most people don't."

Do you reach beyond your finish line? Or are you satisfied when you reach the finish line? The difference is not great; yet it is a giant step. If you will reach beyond your finish line and be a motivator, you can walk your way to the stars.

CONSTANT ACTION

When you become a self-starter, you promise yourself that nothing will stand in your way because you have confidence in yourself, and you cannot be put down. But the promise to yourself also says that you will put this confidence into constant action, for that is the only way goals can be achieved.

An important part of action is the willingness to work hard. During a television interview, I asked Kemmons Wilson, founder of Holiday Inns, if there was a key to his company's success. He replied: "I believe, to be successful, that you have to work at least a half a day—it doesn't make any difference which half, the first twelve hours or the last twelve hours."

TWENTY-EIGHT
Give It All You've Got

Motivation demands that if we are going to succeed in reaching our goals, we should give it all we've got. But far too often we expend only half the energy we should—we do things halfheartedly.

Remember that if someone else is just as capable of reaching your goals as you are, and if you are competing with him, you not only have to give it all you've got, you've got to give it even more than the other person.

ALL YOUR ABILITY
To give a goal all you've got demands a total commitment of devotion, determination, and dedication. You must love what you are striving for with a devotion that never withers. You must feel a dedication to achieve your goals that does not countenance hesitation or doubt.

And you must have a dedication to act that not only manifests outward enthusiasm but also inward enthusiasm and determination.

Devotion is largely a matter of attitude. If you truly believe in your goals, and if they will make you happy and serve others, you should go after them with every ounce of energy you can muster. Without that deep-down desire to achieve, goals will never be reached.

Dedication may be thought of as the highest form of devotion. It focuses on the accomplishments of your goals. It is part and parcel of positive thinking.

I always try to keep moving in a positive *direction*. So often I've been told I couldn't or shouldn't do something, or that I didn't have the talent or the education or experience. Everything negative that is possible to be told has been told to me. But I had dedicated myself to my goals; so had the people who worked with me. We had the same dedication, and "impossible" goals have been reached.

A number of years ago in Elkhart, Kansas, two brothers had a job at the local school. Their task was to get up early every morning and start a fire in the pot-bellied stove in the classroom.

One very cold morning, the brothers cleaned out the stove and loaded it with firewood. The older boy took a can of kerosene and doused the wood with the fuel. With a kitchen match he lit the fire.

The explosion rocked the old building. Due to a delivery man's error, the five-gallon kerosene can had been filled with gasoline. The fire killed the older boy and badly burned the legs of the other.

The doctor who attended to the injured boy told the parents that amputation would be the safest course of action to follow. But the parents were people of determination and faith. They had just lost one son and didn't want to see their other son lose his legs. So they asked the doctor if he couldn't wait just one more day. The doctor said he could.

The next day when the doctor came, the parents asked if he could wait yet another day. And again the next day, they asked for a postponement.

Soon the delay became a week, then a month and more. The parents used the time to instill in the boy the belief that he would walk again someday.

When the bandages were finally removed, it was found that the boy's right leg was two and a half inches shorter than the other. The toes on his left foot had almost been burned off.

Yet, the boy, who was fiercely determined, slowly recovered, going from crutches to walking to running.

He kept running—and those legs that came so close to being amputated carried Glenn Cunningham to a world record in the mile and earned him the title of the "World's Fastest Human Being." Not long ago, Glenn was named athlete of the century at Madison Square Garden. This included all athletes who performed in Madison Square Garden for the first one hundred years. His story is the story of a man who, with determination and indomitable courage beat what seemed to be an overwhelming physical handicap to achieve an "impossible" goal. The obstacles we face in working toward our goals seem small in comparison to those Glenn faced on the road to becoming a world-class runner.

THE VALUE OF COMMITMENT

Honest commitment is invaluable. You should start with some talent, common sense, good judgment, and goals. Then when you have worked out your plan, you've got to dedicate your life to achieving these goals by making an honest commitment that you'll do everything reasonable to achieve them. This takes persistence. And one of the greatest lessons in life is that one cannot walk away and quit. There must be persistence in the face of failure and ridicule. It takes courage and determination to thumb your nose at those people who tell you

you can't do it and to keep going and giving it all you've got. Remember what Yogi Berra achieved after he had been ridiculed.

MORAL COMMITMENT

However, determination and giving it all you've got doesn't mean sacrificing principles. Consider former Arkansas football coach Lou Holtz, now at Notre Dame.

MOTIVATIONAL MEMO
When you think you've given it all you've got, remember: Your best can always be made better.

Lou took the Razorbacks into the Orange Bowl against second-ranked Oklahoma without three of his top players. One was his best running back and another was his best pass receiver. They had been suspended for an alleged campus incident.

The suspension could have cost Arkansas any chance it had against the mighty Sooners, but Lou felt teaching self-respect was more important than winning a ball game.

Despite the controversy, Holtz set about getting his team ready for the game against awesome Oklahoma, which, even before the suspensions, had been favored by eighteen points. But Holtz, as master of motivation, actually turned the underdog status and the suspensions to motivate his team. The result? The underdog Razorbacks ripped the mighty Sooners by eighteen points. The difference wasn't talent—Oklahoma clearly had the better team on paper. The difference was motivation.

BE IN CONTROL

When a car goes down the highway at fifty miles an hour, that is action. But if there is no responsible driver behind the wheel, then there is senseless action.

So it is with your action. Unless you are in control of what you are doing, there is no purpose to it. And there will be no consideration for the rights and well-being of other people.

The motivated person must be in control. He must know himself, his strong points and his weak points. He must know how to approach difficulties, how to conquer failure, how to work and communicate with other people. Yet he must dare to act and to make decisions with conviction that he is not being reckless and inconsiderate of others. His love of people must never be allowed to diminish. And unless there is humility in his achievements, there will be the sin of ego.

There is often a thin line between safe action and unsafe action. Learn to recognize this, and when doubt occurs, slow down, think it through, and ask God for guidance.

ALL YOU'VE GOT—AND MORE

We often think that giving it all we've got is the extent of our abilities. But we can do better than that! What does the runner do? He may be running the ten-mile course and giving it all he's got, but still he comes in third. He's got to do better than that if he wants to win next time. How does he do it? He trains for it. And soon he can do better than he did when he was doing the best he could.

Your best action today need not be your best action tomorrow. And often the extra that is required is not so difficult to obtain.

I was impressed with the philosophy Art Linkletter once shared with me. It summarizes, as well as anything I've read, how you can make your best better:

> Do a little more than you're paid to;
> Give a little more than you have to;
> Try a little harder than you want to;
> Aim a little higher than you think
>   possible;
> And give a lot of thanks to God for
>   health, family, and friends.

TWENTY-NINE
Dare Yourself to Act— Now

You can't hit a home run until you swing the bat.

Results demand action, and goal-oriented people know that action—*action now*—is the only way their goals are going to be achieved.

THE FALLACY OF ABSOLUTE ASSURANCE

People are often tempted to hold off from acting until they are completely sure what the end result will be. In other words, they want assurance of success before they even begin.

This is absolutely wrong. Opportunities come only to motivated people. Thomas Edison did not wait until he knew the secret of the incandescent lamp before he began his experiments. The fact is his experiments had a self-cleansing function: They helped him root out his errors so he could proceed with other avenues of experimentation. He failed thousands of times before he succeeded. Had there been no action, Edison would never have perfected the lamp.

Babe Ruth went into action to set a record on home runs, and at the same time he set a record for striking out. But he knew you can't hit a homer until you swing the bat.

Edison and Ruth are not famous for the number of times they were wrong; they got their fame for the positive things they did. Musicians are not remembered for the hours they spend working out errors during their practice sessions but for the perfection of their performances after they have become masters over their problems; yet it was their errors that helped them perfect their playing.

If we wait for assurance that everything will end successfully, there will never be any action. In a ball game, one side has to win, and the other has to lose. There is no such thing as assurance that both sides will win, and players on any one side do not have assurance that their side will be the winner. Were they to wait for such assurance, there would be no game.

We too have to get into action and use our best talents and try to accomplish our goals.

But what if we fail?

FAILURES BRING SUCCESS

Again, we go back to Thomas Edison and Babe Ruth—both of whom failed while they were trying to set records. But their failures led to success because their failures taught them where improvements were necessary. Had Edison been a negative thinker, we might be using candles today. Had Ruth been a negative thinker, we might never have known his name. But their failures were only temporary ones because these men were positive thinkers, and they used temporary failures to reach their goals.

General Omar Bradley, whose remarkable leadership on the battlefields of Europe won him the greatest devotion from his troops, had this to say about action:

> A second-best decision quickly arrived at and vigorously carried out is better than the best decision too late arrived at and halfheartedly carried out. In everyday affairs, as in battle, we are given one life to live, and the decision is ours whether to wait for circumstances to make up our mind or to act and in acting to live.

THE THERAPY OF ACTION

Perhaps the best way to visualize the value of action is to try to imagine something with no action. Try to think of a ball game, for instance, in which there is no action. The players arrive, but because they can't be 100 percent certain of victory, or because of fear of failure, ridicule, or anxiety they do not play. There is no cheering from the gallery, no scores on the scoreboard. Boredom is so overwhelming that the fans leave—all because nothing happens. Ticket sales are refunded, advertisers cancel their agreements, and what could have been a glorious day filled with excitement and fun has become instead a total washout.

People expect action. It brings out the best in players—the very best—because it is hard, demanding work. And hard work is wonderful therapy.

So it is with you and your goals. Both require hard, demanding work, and if you are not willing to embrace work, your goals can mean nothing to you.

Action is indeed therapy. It erases doubts and fears, anxieties and worry. It capitalizes on failures and mistakes and turns them into positive influences. It exercises the mind for problem solving and for creativity. It develops poise under pressure and uses wisdom and experience to consider alternatives and to provide a backup plan. It calls forth the best in us all, and it becomes the password to success.

Action is work, and work is happiness.

THE DISCIPLINE OF ACTION

There is an educational discipline with action also. It not only points out errors that we should not make again, but it also provides us with valuable guidelines and solutions that we should use over and over. With action we learn our strong points, and we should capitalize on them. A swimmer competing in a free-for-all race may find he does best with the sidestroke or the crawl. Then he should use it if he wishes to win. As you work toward your goals, you will find certain ways of advancing more rapidly, more assuredly. When you do, capitalize on the ways you have found to be successful. Or, if you are a businessman trying to build up sales through mail-order advertising, and you find from experience that a certain kind of ad pulls better than others do, then capitalize on that kind of ad; use it over and over in your future mailings.

> **MOTIVATIONAL MEMO**
> Steps to becoming a man or woman of action: (1) Be a goal setter. (2) Be a self-starter. (3) Give it all you've got. (4) Act *now.*

"Nothing succeeds like success" is an old adage; yet it is true. When you know you have made the right decision, make that same decision again and again when like situations come up. This is the way a doctor works when treating a patient; if the patient responds to a certain kind of medicine, the doctor will continue that medication until the patient's health is restored. That is purposeful action.

EXAMPLES OF SUCCESSFUL ACTION

Successful action may be thought of as action that reaches a happy conclusion.

There is a story of Pete Gray, who, at the age of six, lost his arm in a farming accident. When he tried to jump on a slow-moving wagon, he fell off, catching his right arm in the wheel spokes. The arm, badly damaged, had to be amputated above the elbow.

Despite this apparently overwhelming obstacle, Pete set a seemingly unattainable goal for himself. His dream? To play major league baseball.

Though right-handed, he learned to bat from the left side. By concentrating all his efforts on that side, he strengthened his left arm. He had a great batting eye, mixing sharp liners with perfectly laid down bunts. He could also hit for distance—doubles, triples, and even home runs.

Even more amazing was his ability to field. He wore his glove, padding removed, on his fingertips. After catching the ball, he would stick the glove under the stump of his right arm, grab the ball with his left hand and throw, losing very little time. Gray played on semi-pro teams for years.

While playing at Memphis, Pete Gray began to receive national attention. In 1944 he hit .333, stole sixty-three bases, and was named the league's Most Valuable Player. In two seasons with the Chicks, he struck out just fifteen times. The U.S. government made films of Pete to show to wounded veterans.

In 1945 Pete Gray's dream came true when he signed with the American League champion, the St. Louis Browns. Gray had reached his goal despite a handicap that would have stopped almost anyone else. He did it through motivation, determination, and action—through giving it all he had.

ACTION AND MOTIVATION

Disraeli once said that action may not always bring happiness, but there is no happiness without action. To this I would add that action does bring satisfaction—even in those instances where action does not bring happiness. For motivation is the key to the achievement of goals, and even if you give 100 percent action and for some reason your goal is not reached, there is immense satisfaction in knowing that you worked to the best of your ability to reach it and that you learned something and are better for the experience.

If you have goals that burn with a desire to be fulfilled, you then have the motivation to act, and action is the only way they will be fulfilled. The only way to a successful life is to make your own. It is like rafting in white water; you must keep paddling or you'll end up on the rocks.

THIRTY
I Challenge You to Improve Your Life

At the beginning of this book, we discussed how motivation can work miracles in your life, can help you to reach your goals, can cause you to attain growth and happiness, for it is motivation that inspires you to take action to realize your dreams.

As you've read this book, I hope you've found some information that will be personally helpful to you as you set out to reach your goals, some spark that will ignite the fire of motivation within you.

The world is full of opportunities waiting to be seized. And, as you've seen, new ones turn up everyday. But the key to making the most of those opportunities is *action*. What if some of the people you've read about had failed to act on their ideas? This country wouldn't be what it is today. Dream your dreams, but *motivate yourself* to put your plans into motion. Have the courage to act on your ideas, for in doing so, you will be on your way to achieving your goals in life.

I challenge you to take action, *right now!* You've read about how others did it, and now it's your turn. Decide this very day to be the best you can be. Get up right now, get a pencil and paper, set down your goals, and create a personal plan of action to get what you want out of life. Don't settle for less—give it all you've got!

Life is not only a challenge and an opportunity, but life is also pain, tears, and failure. Yet in order to get what you want from life, you must overcome these things and go for your goals with all the enthusiasm you can muster. Sure, there are risks involved when you say yes to life and decide to reach for goals you may have never dreamed you could achieve. Sure, there are disappointments and setbacks along the way. But your life is a journey only you can take if you want to become the best person you can be.

You are a rare and special human being; since the beginning of time, billions of people have walked the earth, but there never has been and there never will be another you. And because you are unique, only you can develop your special talents. You will need help, but only you can take the action to carry out the plan the Creator has for you. So thank God for life and ask for His help in using your abilities to become what He wants you to become. You are His child; just as you want the best for your children, so He wants the best for you. You can do no less than give your best back to Him.

Thank God for life and ask His guidance in using your abilities and talents to become what He wants you to become.

Remember, you are a special person. Give life your very best and be proud to be you!

The Success Seekers Easy Index

The Action Index to Successful People

Other Living Books Best-sellers

ANSWERS by Josh McDowell and Don Stewart. In a question-and-answer format, the authors tackle sixty-five of the most-asked questions about the Bible, God, Jesus Christ, miracles, other religions, and Creation. 07-0021-X

THE BELOVED STRANGER by Grace Livingston Hill. Graham came into her life at a desperate time, then vanished. But Sherrill could not forget the handsome stranger who captured her heart. 07-0303-0

BUILDING YOUR SELF-IMAGE by Josh McDowell and Don Stewart. Here are practical answers to help you overcome your fears, anxieties, and lack of self-confidence. Learn how God's higher image of who you are can take root in your heart and mind. 07-1395-8

THE CHILD WITHIN by Mari Hanes. The author shares insights she gained from God's Word during her own pregnancy, identifying areas of stress, offering concrete data about the birth process, and pointing to God's promises to lead those who are with young. 07-0219-0

COME BEFORE WINTER AND SHARE MY HOPE by Charles R. Swindoll. A collection of brief vignettes offering hope and the assurance that adversity and despair are temporary setbacks we can overcome! 07-0477-0

DR. DOBSON ANSWERS YOUR QUESTIONS by Dr. James Dobson. In this convenient reference book, renowned author Dr. James Dobson addresses heartfelt concerns on many topics, including marital relationships, infant care, child discipline, home management, and others. 07-0580-7

THE EFFECTIVE FATHER by Gordon MacDonald. A practical study of effective fatherhood based on biblical principles. 07-0669-2

FOR WOMEN ONLY by Evelyn R. and J. Allan Petersen. This balanced, entertaining, and diversified treatment covers all the aspects of womanhood. 07-0897-0

HOW TO BE HAPPY THOUGH MARRIED by Tim LaHaye. A valuable resource that tells how to develop physical , mental, and spiritual harmony in marriage. 07-1499-7

Other Living Books Best-sellers

JOHN, SON OF THUNDER by Ellen Gunderson Traylor. In this saga of adventure, romance, and discovery, travel with John—the disciple whom Jesus loved—down desert paths, through the courts of the Holy City, and to the foot of the cross as he leaves his luxury as a privileged son of Israel for the bitter hardship of his exile on Patmos. 07-1903-4

LIFE IS TREMENDOUS! by Charlie "Tremendous" Jones. Believing that enthusiasm makes the difference, Jones shows how anyone can be happy, involved, relevant, productive, healthy, and secure in the midst of a high-pressure, commercialized society. 07-2184-5

MORE THAN A CARPENTER by Josh McDowell. A hard-hitting book for people who are skeptical about Jesus' deity, his resurrection, and his claim on their lives. 07-4552-3

QUICK TO LISTEN, SLOW TO SPEAK by Robert E. Fisher. Families are shown how to express love to one another by developing better listening skills, finding ways to disagree without arguing, and using constructive criticism. 07-5111-6

REASONS by Josh McDowell and Don Stewart. In a convenient question-and-answer format, the authors address many of the commonly asked questions about the Bible and evolution. 07-5287-2

RUTH, A LOVE STORY by Ellen Gunderson Traylor. Though the pain of separation and poverty would come upon her, Ruth was to become part of the very fulfillment of prophecy—and find true love as well. A biblical novel. 07-5809-9

THE SECRET OF LOVING by Josh McDowell. McDowell explores the values and qualities that will help both the single and married reader to be the right person for someone else. 07-5845-5

THE STORY FROM THE BOOK. From Adam to Armageddon, this book captures the full sweep of the Bible's content in abridged, chronological form. Based on *The Book*, the best-selling, popular edition of *The Living Bible*. 07-6677-6

Other Living Books Best-sellers

THE STRONG-WILLED CHILD by Dr. James Dobson. With practical solutions and humorous anecdotes, Dobson shows how to discipline an assertive child without breaking his spirit. Parents will learn to overcome feelings of defeat or frustration by setting boundaries and taking action. 07-5924-9

SUCCESS! THE GLENN BLAND METHOD by Glenn Bland. The author shows how to set goals and make plans that really work. His ingredients for success include spiritual, financial, educational, and recreational balances. 07-6689-X

THROUGH GATES OF SPLENDOR by Elisabeth Elliot. This unforgettable story of five men who braved the Auca Indians has become one of the most famous missionary books of all time. 07-7151-6

WHAT WIVES WISH THEIR HUSBANDS KNEW ABOUT WOMEN by James Dobson. The best-selling author of *Dare to Discipline* and *The Strong-Willed Child* brings us this vital book that speaks to the unique emotional needs and aspirations of today's woman. An immensely practical, interesting guide. 07-7896-0

WHY YOU ACT THE WAY YOU DO by Tim LaHaye. Discover how your temperament affects your work, emotions, spiritual life, and relationships, and learn how to make improvements. 07-8212-7